CW01022679

In this book Richard Evans [...] emotional literacy actually [...] everyday life. Moreover, he p[...] spective and demystifies th[...] and very readable way.

The book provides a clear, structured and practical outlook on what the conversation between a school and its pupils should be like, and how this conversation can be refined and made more effective for the benefit of all.

Independent Thinking on Emotional Literacy is a must-read for anyone who works with young people; any school that follows Richard's advice will be confident that they possess a clear grasp of the voice of their pupils, and will be making major steps to reduce any disaffection or disengagement.

PETER NELMES, SCHOOL LEADER AND AUTHOR OF
TROUBLED HEARTS, TROUBLED MINDS: MAKING SENSE
OF THE EMOTIONAL DIMENSION OF LEARNING

Independent Thinking on Emotional Literacy offers a vivid and realistic account of the lives of many students and gets to the heart of why some students are simply not in a place to learn when they arrive at school. It is written in a very honest and down-to-earth manner, and provides a range of helpful examples of some of the key challenges students often face when they struggle with their emotional literacy. Furthermore, the introduction of the passport is a helpful and relatively simple tool for practitioners to use as a focus for the not-so-simple process of supporting pupils to successfully and independently develop their emotional literacy skills.

NATALIE PACKER, EDUCATION CONSULTANT
ON SEND AND SCHOOL IMPROVEMENT

I would recommend *Independent Thinking on Emotional Literacy* to anyone wanting practical ways to address what is often a difficult area in an already crowded curriculum – that of pupils' emotional literacy.

Writing in a highly engaging manner, Richard offers himself as a guide, provides a licence to travel on the journey (presented in the form of the passport) and encourages educators to explore how they can better navigate the territory that is the inner emotional world of their pupils. The passport itself is a powerful tool to assist in engaging pupils in meaningful discussions that will help develop their self-efficacy, motivation and specific skills for successfully engaging in the world of school.

All in all, *Independent Thinking on Emotional Literacy* is an invaluable resource for any teacher or mentor working in a wide variety of educational settings.

STEVE RUSSELL, BEHAVIOUR, LEADERSHIP AND WELL-BEING CONSULTANT

Independent Thinking on Emotional Literacy is essential reading for all staff who want to support young people to become happy, confident adults, and not just knowledgeable ones. The generosity, empathy and patience that we need to show in order for this to happen can seem daunting, but Richard Evans offers practical and effective advice on what questions to ask, how to ask them and – most importantly – how to listen to the answers. It is becoming increasingly clear that young people need ever more support in reaching a level of emotional understanding that will allow them to succeed both in school and beyond – and, in an engaging way that will speak to all teachers, Richard shows us how we can help.

JOSEPHINE ROCHFORD, TEACHER OF ENGLISH, MONK'S WALK SCHOOL

Richard Evans' *Independent Thinking on Emotional Literacy* is exactly what we have been waiting for in schools. Everyone is acutely aware, now more than ever, that teaching emotional literacy is one of the most important things we can do to help a child's sense of well-being and future success – and it is also well known that emotionally literate children perform better in school. But how do we teach it? Cue Richard to the rescue, as his vast experience of tutoring nurture groups and his sense of humour make reading the book feel like you are chatting with a good friend. He pulls together a range of theoretical perspectives and offers plenty of suggestions on how to develop students' independent thinking in order to help them find solutions for each scenario around the passport, which can also be adapted to suit your own setting.

Essential reading for anyone passionate about helping children and young people become more emotionally literate.

PAULA REEVES, EMOTIONAL LITERACY LEAD, BROOKE HILL ACADEMY

Independent Thinking on Emotional Literacy is an excellent read which is honest, accessible and captures you from the start. It offers both new and experienced colleagues something rather unique, and builds upon the fundamental need for our children to understand themselves – illustrating that if we get this right, the rest will follow.

The passport is a potential game changer for pupils and teachers alike, offering teachers the means with which to increase their pupils' confidence, engagement, resilience and learning. It provides us with a 'how to' and encourages educators to find their own way with it – to use it, adapt it and grow it. Furthermore, it breaks resilience down into measurable behaviours and allows students to identify their own needs and to be reflective in their progress. This highlights an asset-focused approach to all things well-being – to focus on what we can bring into our lives and the changes we can make.

The book is startlingly accurate in its description of transition and the whirlwind start to the academic year for pupils and teachers alike, reminding us of the power of listening and the importance of making time in our work with pupils and in education. It also made me laugh out loud in parts and deeply reflect in others.

Independent Thinking on Emotional Literacy has significantly added key insights to my 20 years' experience of teaching, pastoral leadership and work with young people. Thank you, Richard, for reminding me to keep thinking and reading to improve my own practice!

LYNETTE HARTE, SCHOOL LIAISON, RESILIENT RUTLAND

INDEPENDENT
THINKING
ON ...

EMOTIONAL LITERACY

Richard Evans

A PASSPORT TO INCREASED CONFIDENCE,
ENGAGEMENT AND LEARNING

independent
thinking press

First published by

Independent Thinking Press
Crown Buildings, Bancyfelin, Carmarthen, Wales, SA33 5ND, UK
www.independentthinkingpress.com

and

Independent Thinking Press
PO Box 2223, Williston, VT 05495, USA
www.crownhousepublishing.com

Independent Thinking Press is an imprint of Crown House Publishing Ltd.

Edited by Ian Gilbert.

The Independent Thinking On ... series is typeset in Azote, Buckwheat TC Sans,
Cormorant Garamond and Montserrat.

The Independent Thinking On ... series cover style was designed by Tania Willis
www.taniawillis.com.

British Library Cataloguing-in-Publication Data
A catalogue entry for this book is available from the British Library.

Print ISBN 978-178135373-8
Mobi ISBN 978-178135378-3
ePub ISBN 978-178135379-0
ePDF ISBN 978-178135380-6

LCCN 2020945095

Printed and bound in the UK by
Gomer Press, Llandysul, Ceredigion

For mum and dad – because you couldn't have shown more love to more people.

FOREWORD

I was once gifted a book entitled *Could Do Better: School Reports of the Great and the Good*.[1] It was an entertaining compendium of teacher comments stretching back for over a century – from 'He cannot be trusted to behave himself anywhere'[2] (Winston Churchill) and 'He has glaring faults and they have certainly glared at us this term'[3] (Stephen Fry) to 'She must try to be less emotional in her dealing with others'[4] (Princess Diana) and 'All glib and cleverness'[5] (Carl Gustav Jung).

Although good for a chuckle, these comments show how subjective, inaccurate, meaningless and unhelpful this way of reporting on a young person's potential really is.

Of course, we have come a long way since a teacher could write, 'He shows great originality, which must be curbed at all times'[6] (Peter Ustinov) and get away with it – and reporting is usually done in a more humane, collaborative and productive manner these days.

Or is it?

To what extent do we enter into a genuine dialogue with young people, whether it's with the academic high-flyers or those making their way through school rather closer to the ground? Do we really engage with our students, not only in a conversation about what they are doing wrong and what they should be doing instead, but one that

---

1   C. Hurley (ed), *Could Do Better: School Reports of the Great and the Good* (London: Simon and Schuster, 1997).

2   Ibid, p. 98.

3   Ibid, p. 42.

4   Ibid, p. 136.

5   Ibid, p. 138.

6   Ibid, p. 25.

actually helps equip them with the tools and approaches that will be of real help as they chase the almost mythical 'do better' goal?

Even the schools that are dogmatically following Rosenshine's Principles of instruction – with its focus on review, small steps, scaffolding, questioning and the like – might be missing something more fundamental when it comes to helping young people improve.[7] And that something is at an emotional rather than purely technical or cognitive level – and it is that emotional understanding, and the way it can hinder or help classroom attainment, that is at the heart of this book.

Of course, the idea of emotional intelligence has been around for quite a while since it first appeared in academic papers in the 1960s, but it was well and truly brought to the fore by the science writer Daniel Goleman in his seminal book *Emotional Intelligence*.[8] For a brief, some may say glorious time, we knew that there was more to getting ahead than IQ and that our EQ had a big part to play in how we effectively thought about ourselves and those around us. And of course, that is still the case. The World Economic Forum's 2018 research into the most sought-after skills for 2022 has 'emotional intelligence' as number eight in its list of 'trending' skills, just below 'leadership and social influence' but above 'reasoning, problem-solving and ideation'.[9] (Worth noting here too is that its list of skills in global decline include 'memory,

---

7 B. Rosenshine, Principles of instruction: research-based strategies that all teachers should know, *American Educator*, 36(1) (2012): 12-19, 39.

8 D. Goleman, *Emotional Intelligence: Why It Can Matter More Than IQ* (London: Bloomsbury, 1996).

9 World Economic Forum, *The Future of Jobs Report 2018* (Insight Report) (Geneva: World Economic Forum, 2018), p. 12. Available at: http://www3weforum.org/docs/WEF_Future_of_Jobs_2018.pdf.

verbal, auditory and spatial abilities' and 'reading, writing, math and active listening'. Hey, don't shoot the messenger.)

What happened in our schools, though, was the state-driven ideological hijack both of the curriculum and the pedagogy employed to teach it. The kings and queens retook their thrones from hoi polloi such as Social and Emotional Aspects of Learning (SEAL) and Every Child Matters, while group work, teamwork and Personalised Learning and Thinking Skills (PLTS) were unceremoniously thrown in a school skip in favour of direct transmission and didactic teaching with a zero-tolerance approach to any child who took it upon themselves to kick off. What this meant was that those espousing that we seek to under-stand, even love, a child (and not simply manipulate them) were dismissed as tree-hugging sentimentalists whose 'soft expectations' would assign a generation of unquali-fied young people to a life working in low-paid jobs, as opposed to the generation we have now of highly quali-fied young people working in low-paid jobs and up to their necks in debt.[10] And that was before factoring in the dev-astating effects of the 2020 COVID-19 pandemic on the graduate job market.[11]

Fortunately, there are still many teachers who, to borrow an old saw, prefer to be teaching children rather than sim-ply teaching subjects – and so the focus on using understandings, strategies and practices from the world of emotional intelligence has prevailed, albeit under the radar of Ofsted and under the noses of school managers

---

10 K. Makortoff, UK Employers Will Offer Fewer Entry-Level Jobs in 2020, Figures Suggest, *The Guardian* (6 January 2020). Available at: https://www.theguardian.com/money/2020/jan/06/uk-employers-fewer-entry-level-jobs-2020-survey.

11 Institute of Student Employers (ISE), Graduate Jobs Decline in 21 Countries Due to Covid-19, *FE News* (15 July 2020). Available at: https://www.fenews.co.uk/press-releases/51463-graduate-jobs-decline-in-21-countries-due-to-covid-19.

who are more inclined to use students to improve their data rather than the other way round.

And Richard Evans is one such practitioner.

Drawn from his direct experience of working with troubled and troublesome young people, Richard has shown how asking the right questions in the right way and at the right time pays dividends in helping those young people get back on track and stay there.

By working to understand them – and help them to understand themselves – at a more emotional level, we can all help our students develop the necessary emotional intelligence to excel not only at school but beyond. In this way we genuinely help them create a passport to a better, more fulfilled life. Which is perhaps of greater use than simply expressing regret that the 'threat of failure in his exams has not helped him to grow out of a tediously lackadaisical unsupportiveness' (Jeremy Paxman).[12]

IAN GILBERT
WEST WALES

---

12 Hurley, *Could Do Better*, p. 56.

ACKNOWLEDGEMENTS

So none of this would have happened without the collaboration of Bernie and the many brilliant students and staff who trialled and informed the passport, nor without the backing and encouragement of key senior leaders – you all know who you are.

Or, indeed, those friends and family who generously read, checked and advised: Angela, Freddie, Grace, Laurence, Liz, Mark, Mel, Oliver and Paul.

And it definitely wouldn't have happened without Ian's guidance and quietly blazing care, or without Emma's skilful eye or the patient teamwork of those at Crown House Publishing.

Thank you to Clare for taking on more caring so I could do more writing; to Cathy for her relentless ideas and resources; to Jane for her drive and compassion for all.

Way back, there was Deborah's immortal advice: 'If the job doesn't exist, create it'; Jacob's conviction: 'There's a book in you, write it'; and Amit's recognition of needs: not just the passport's, but my own.

But it still wouldn't have happened without Freddie, Grace, Oliver or Mel: the people who make me feel loved and inspired, who push me to think, who are always there for me.

Nor without those who have been my role models since as long as I can remember: my mum, dad and sisters. Thank you to you all.

CONTENTS

FIRST THOUGHTS

A friend of mine, let's call her Google, tells me people often ask her what emotional literacy means. This friend – intelligent, well-connected – says it describes a person's ability to understand and express feelings. She says not only does it involve being self-aware and managing your own feelings – for example, by staying calm when you're angry – but also being sensitive, and able to adapt, to the feelings of others.[1]

I tell her I like her definition. Not least because it points to the idea that these two words were meant for each other. Emotions are raw and savage, I offer, with a backstory to tell. Being literate in something is about having knowledge and understanding, in order that conundrums can be solved. Emotions and literacy feel like they belong together.

I might have misjudged the terms of our friendship because she's already onto something else. No time for chat or reflection. So I leave her be, to her world of Q&As, and toss these thoughts around in my head.

And my thoughts go to education. I wonder if the strength of our determination for our children to be conventionally schooled and skilled means that we overlook a more fundamental educational need: for our children to understand themselves. I even wonder if, in trying so earnestly to push a knowledge curriculum, we inadvertently crush opportunities for this more primal form of learning to take place.

Independent Thinking on Emotional Literacy is the result of these thoughts. It is an attempt to explore the emotional grey areas between the education system and the

---

1   See https://www.specialeducationalneeds.co.uk/emotional literacy.html.

pupil. In it, you will be taken on a tour of the world of the pupil. Not because you don't know about it – you pretty much wrote the manual – but because it's good to be reminded. And also because you already have your hands full with the demands of your own world.

You will be reminded of your pupils' weaknesses and inhibitions; of their quirks and habits; of their upbringings and predispositions; of their needs and ambitions; of their innocence and strengths. And alongside this, you will be given a ready-made tool (well, a sheet of paper, but you know what I mean) with which to unpick, and hopefully help to enhance, the world of your pupil – in order that they can have better experiences of, at and, indeed, after school.

This tool, this sheet of A3, is called the passport.[2] Like the traditional travel document, it's designed to get you into new territories that will broaden your horizons, albeit with a few officious glares and refusals to enter along the way.

Through the language of feelings and needs (and a good dose of highlighter therapy), the passport enables staff to steer young people to greater emotional understanding of themselves, so they can better manage their route through the unwieldy school system. The passport is like an old-fashioned map: you faff with it until it's the right way around, plot your course together, make marks where you need and, in unequal measures of harmony and conflict, you find a way through.

It isn't aimed at any particular member of staff, student or educational setting. I've run with it at secondary level but it's just as welcome at primary and in further education. We feel and have needs at all ages. To unpick them, with compassion, is relevant to all.

---

2 Colour copies of the passport can be downloaded for free from: https://www.crownhouse.co.uk/featured/emotional-literacy.

If it's aimed at anyone, adult or child, it's those not altogether happy with the system; those not convinced it provides as much breadth and meaning as it could; who question whether enough teaching is getting to enough children; who sense that education is as much about the acquisition of self-knowledge as it is about that of knowledge per se.

You will have questions. I shall try to answer them. But not right away. We need to hold our horses a little and take stock of our existing set-up: at the realities of everyday school life; at what works and is so impressive about education; at what malfunctions and is ripe for improvement. And then we can get going on this passport thing, this tool-like sheet of A3, to see if it can help.

You hold the map; I'll lead the way. I hope you've not forgotten the Werther's.

CHAPTER 1
WHIRLWIND

You've got your new uniform but the trousers don't fit. The jacket's too big and your tie's askew. And a foot too long. One of hundreds, you are, seeping in through the gates of your new learning centre. Self-conscious, anxious, directionless, but for the tide of uniform that carries you forward towards, well, wherever it is you're meant to start. Desperately looking for anyone who might constitute a new friend, someone assigned to the same place you've been assigned to, wherever that is. Someone of similar height, look, fear, confusion.

Were there space, last night would be replaying its familiar sequences in your head. How many times was it you awoke? Older brother next door, younger sister next bed, phone ping, worry dream, covers off, covers on, knees up, knees down, face plant. Do you need a PE kit? Did dad remember to pick up the tie? Whose house do you go to this weekend? And why have you started making odd vocal noises out loud for no reason, skipping slightly before each stride, tapping your leg repeatedly on the table?

But your head doesn't have space. This is too all-consuming. Teachers are barking out instructions, kids falling in and out of line, voices booming, silences, racket, then silence again. And then at some point, you end up in a room with a load of other lost souls, barely listening to a word that is being projected by the figure at the front. Instead, you fidget with your bag, your pencil, your desk, your hands, with anything in fact that you can lay those same hands on, to somehow stop the worry and the fear and the confusion, the loneliness and the conundrum that is, right now, the thoroughly unwelcome institution of school.

Fast forward a month, a term, and some of this anxiety has eased: your timetable is either scribbled in your planner or etched on your memory – or you've just become good at following people. Your trousers still don't fit but you've semi-grown into your jacket; teachers scare you less; you have a friend or two; your tie now stops at your trousers.

Only to be replaced, however, by a wealth of supplementary worries, of unexpected stresses – such as homework and deadlines; seating and equipment; concentration and behaviour.

How to steer your way through it? Teachers, of course, are the ones charged with that task. And, by and large, they do their utmost to do so. With whichever tools are available. In whatever time. While juggling the known and unknown quantities of their own daily realities – you know, the meetings, the targets, the marking, the behaviour, the last-minute cover lessons, the marriage breakdowns, the photocopier. Regardless, you'll likely have at least one story about one teacher who did the steering, the caring and the inspiring so well that it still resounds years later; a teacher to whom you feel you owe so much. The one who realised something the others didn't, who picked you out of the crowd to make your business their business. The one who did something you had no idea at the time would echo for years to come. The one who helped make you you: your Mr Al-Hawi, my Mrs Whiting; your Mrs Yun, my Mr Keats.

We've all watched those teachers. The ones in control but not dominating, listening but not paying lip service; the ones praising but not patronising, reprimanding but not humiliating; the ones teaching but not lecturing, loving but not spoiling. And we've all watched their students –

those learning, not idling; growing, not stagnating; those feeling inspired, not bored.

Behind many good teachers are, of course, good schools. Not Ofsted-good necessarily – whatever that means at the time of writing – but good good. Those varying their curriculum; those coaching staff to provide it; those counselling and mentoring, advising and strategising; those opening early and closing late, informing and preparing, alerting and reminding, smiling and staying positive; those who know that to care about the parent and carer is to care about the child.

And behind every good school is a wealth of adults throwing their all behind the cause: the teachers and teaching assistants; the office staff and estates people; the IT gurus and technicians; the kitchen staff, cleaners and caretakers; the governors and parent volunteers. Every single contributing adult whose delirious dedication and slagheap of paid and unpaid hours (12.1 hours a week at last count – the highest of all UK workers[1]) means that at least some of the above can be achieved on behalf of the pupils. Whatever the success rate, effectiveness or overall value of a school, whatever anyone makes of any individual place of education, that incontrovertible reality of every educational institution is simply not to be sniffed at: schools exist, and sometimes even prosper, because the adults who work within them do so because they care. And some.

But for all this, schools still have an uncanny knack of not always working for their pupils. For one, great numbers of

---

1   TUC analysis of official statistics using unpublished Office for National Statistics data from the Labour Force Survey (July–September 2018) and the Annual Survey of Hours and Earnings (2018): Workers in the UK put in more than £32 billion worth of unpaid overtime last year [press release] (1 March 2019). Available at: https://www.tuc.org.uk/news/workers-uk-put-more-£32-billion-worth-unpaid-overtime-last-year-tuc-analysis.

them are falling short of expected standards. According to the exams regulator Ofqual, in England in 2019, across all subjects taken, nearly one in three GCSE pupils failed to achieve the expected standard of pass, recording Grade 3s or below – a 'failure' rate which remains broadly the same year-on-year.[2] Of course, this also means that nigh on 70% of exams taken were passed, but try asking for congratulation cards from those who took the 30% that weren't.

In view of these numbers, we perhaps shouldn't be surprised when we also learn that, underpinning this underachievement (underachievement in the Department of Education's judgement, at least) is a plethora of unhappy – and, we can surely infer, demotivated – children. As part of a 2017 PISA report, around one in six 15-year-olds said they were 'not satisfied with life', ranking UK pupils 38th out of 48 countries from which the data was collected.[3] And if that's a little too 15-year-old-centric, there is plenty of broader evidence of student malcontent from other age sets: according to a 2017 report by the mental health charity Young Minds, every classroom has three children with 'a diagnosable mental health problem',[4] and the Children Society's annual *Good Childhood* report describes as 'really concerning' the figures that suggest about a

2 Ofqual, Guide to GCSE results for England, 2019 [press release] (22 August 2019). Available at: https://www.gov.uk/government/news/guide-to-gcse-results-for-england-2019.

3 OECD, *PISA 2015 Results (Volume III): Students' Well-being* (Paris: OECD Publishing, 2017), p. 11. Available at: https://www.oecd.org/pisa/PISA-2015-Results-Students-Well-being-Volume-III-Overview.pdf. See also H. Ward, New Pisa happiness table: see where UK pupils rank, *TES* (19 April 2017). Available at: https://www.tes.com/news/new-pisa-happiness-table-see-where-uk-pupils-rank; and H. French, What are we doing to our children?, *The Telegraph* (10 October 2017). Available at: https://www.telegraph.co.uk/education/2017/10/10/children1.

4 A. Cowburn and M. Blow, *Wise Up: Prioritising Wellbeing in Schools* (London: Young Minds, 2017), p. 2. Available at: https://youngminds.org.uk/media/1428/wise-up-prioritising-wellbeing-in-schools.pdf.

quarter of a million children, aged between 10 and 17, 'could now be unhappy with their lives' – the worst recorded result since 2009.[5]

Several steps beyond unhappy, I guess, is not being at school altogether. Government statistics for the 2017–2018 period tell us that one in every thousand pupils (across primary, secondary and special education) were excluded that year – make that two per thousand for secondary miscreants.[6] What's more, where exclusion presumably wouldn't suit the image of the school in question, there is also now (or perhaps it's been going on for years) the option of 'off-rolling' – recognised by Ofsted as 'the practice of removing a pupil from the school roll without a formal, permanent exclusion or by encouraging a parent to remove their child from the school roll, when the removal is primarily in the interests of the school rather than in the best interests of the pupil'.[7]

Despite the government's noble assertion in 2003 that 'every child matters',[8] we seem to have realised since that, well, actually, on reflection, they don't. Or maybe just can't. In 2017, researchers from the Education Policy Institute (EPI) found that around one in twelve pupils in the UK who were due to sit their GCSEs that year were mysteriously removed from the rolls – no explanation provided. According to the EPI, 'as many as 8.1 per cent of [Year 11s

---

5   Children's Society, *The Good Childhood Report 2019*, p. 5. Available at: https://www.childrenssociety.org.uk/sites/default/files/the_good_childhood_report_2019.pdf.

6   Department for Education, Permanent and fixed period exclusions in England: 2017 to 2018 (25 July 2019). Available at: https://assets.publishing.service.gov.uk/government/uploads/system/uploads/attachment_data/file/820773/Permanent_and_fixed_period_exclusions_2017_to_2018_-_main_text.pdf.

7   See https://www.gov.uk/government/publications/off-rolling-exploring-the-issue.

8   Chief Secretary to the Treasury, *Every Child Matters*, Cm. 5860 (London: TSO, 2003). Available at: https://www.gov.uk/government/publications/every-child-matters.

that year] were subject to moves that cannot be accounted for'.[9] With the majority of those pupils representing our most vulnerable groups, some commentators have been minded to wonder whether, for some pupils at least, the proximity of their exams and the meagreness of their predicted grades were in any way related to the mystery of their disappearances.

And while we're talking about students who seem to vanish into thin air – if you've worked in a school, you probably know one – the increasingly popular practice of home-schooling might be behind it. The BBC found that 48,000 children were being home educated in 2016–2017, which constituted an increase of around 40% from 2014–2015.[10] Regardless of its efficacy as a replacement education, which I imagine ranges on a scale of 'Thank goodness I got out of that place and can actually work and succeed in peace – thank you' to 'Home what?', we should at least acknowledge that the conventional system is not working for a small but increasingly significant proportion of our young people.

But why on earth, you might wonder, would a system with so much money earnestly poured into it – a cool £91 billion in 2018–2019, according to the Institute for Fiscal Studies[11] – and so many willing workers and volunteers assigned to it, not expect to produce a more happy, inclusive, attractive

9   J. Hutchinson and W. Crenna-Jennings, *Unexplained Pupil Exits from Schools: A Growing Problem?* Working paper (April) (London: Education Policy Institute, 2019). Available at: https://epi.org.uk/wp-content/uploads/2019/04/EPI_Unexplained-pupil-exits_2019.pdf.

10 M. Issimdar, Homeschooling in the UK increases 40% over three years, *BBC News* (26 April 2018). Available at: https://www.bbc.co.uk/news/uk-england-42624220.

11 J. Britton, C. Farquharson and L. Sibieta, *2019 Annual Report on Education Spending in England* (London: Institute for Fiscal Studies, 2019), p. 6. Available at: https://www.ifs.org.uk/uploads/R162-Education-spending-in-England-2019.pdf.

and grade-attaining education for its young guests? How is it that a system can provide so much but, in far too many cases, yield so little?

Because, I would argue, it doesn't provide the foundation on which every progressive school education depends: the development of pupils' *emotional intelligence* to identify and solve the unspoken issues of school. Why don't I ever put my hand up? Why do I always call out? Why don't I do my homework? Why don't teachers like me? Without the emotional dexterity to solve the age-old problems they experience at school, at best pupils are not in a position to properly benefit from all it has to offer, and at worst they withdraw and are lost.

School life, and all that it entails, demands emotional literacy – it is this that should be pupils' first piece of equipment, their first item of uniform. Before any staff member has even picked up a whiteboard pen or created a class register, the first item on every school's agenda should be this: what can we put in place to develop our pupils' emotional intelligence? And if we can't help them all (or they don't all need helping), who should we start with?

Why? Because the reality is that many kids are so caught up in the whirlwind of school, home and all the baggage that resides in-between, that what schools sincerely provide sometimes barely even touches the sides.

How do you even start to master school when you can barely master yourself? When you've not yet worked out how to look after a worksheet. When you're still trying to remember to bring in your lunch. When you're always tired at school because you can't sleep at night. When you can't remember to take in your homework. When you don't know how to do it. When other children are clearly more popular. When you feel lonely and bullied and different in a way that the school powers that be, the dominant minority, won't forgive. When you start each school day being nagged or undermined or both – even though you think you're doing your best. When you feel like you're failing. When you're scared and falling. How would anyone, when such situations are tightening their grip, stealthily like flu germs, be ready to learn?

But school is the wheel that just keeps on turning. Alarms keep going off, uniforms thrown on, breakfasts wolfed, doors slammed, registers taken, homework rushed, assemblies delivered, lessons started, titles underlined, dates scribbled, hands raised, hands retracted, answers given, answers avoided, praise afforded, reprimands issued, shouting resisted, shouting succumbed to. In short, pupils keep being pupils and teachers keep being teachers.

And those bells ... those bells that keep raucously interrupting whatever it is that happens to be going on in the classroom at the time, to signify the end of each lesson, the end of that episode of learning or enduring, and the blaring, urgent roll call to another destination of more learning or enduring, or, in some cases, resisting and wrecking, or even giving up. Someone, somewhere, has to quit with the campanology obsession and ease up on those bells, at least for a time.

Time enough to freeze-frame what is happening, to stun-gun our young people and free the characters from their shells. Time enough to transport them out of that classroom and show them their learning life. Time enough, Scrooge and his spirits style, to walk them through the ghosts of their educational past and present (future maybe another time). Time enough to start to unpick what is happening and what can be provided, what can be learned in the life of an everyday pupil. So when the characters do walk back into their shells, and the bells start ringing again, theirs is a lesson worth going to, a lunch-time worth sitting down for, a school worth attending, an education worth being educated for, because now they are a pupil with more self-knowledge and, by conse-quence, more self-worth. And education, in all its guises, can begin.

CHAPTER 2

LEARNING TO LISTEN

The passport started life as a conversation between two teachers in a little room overlooking a big field. Two teachers employed by one school to deliver personalised lessons to small groups of students. So small you couldn't call them a group. So lost you could barely call some students. Instead of teaching thirty-two, we were tasked with teaching two. At a time. So much freedom, we didn't know what to do with ourselves.

So we talked ... and the conversation centred around what it was to be an able pupil. Not just able, but one of the ones who sail through their education, picking up facts and figures, certificates and commendations, grades and distinctions. More stature and maturity at the end of it, with barely a hair out of place, a bead of sweat perspired.

And then we moved to something more grounded, more tangible: what do the pupils who cope best with school actually do? At school. At home. And in-between. What exactly does a 'coper' look like? This question led to one of the most interesting discussions I have had in teaching because it tried to home in on the unspoken issues of school – the ones that are the traits of the pupil who copes best. And the more we thought about it, the more we wondered why we so rarely talk meaningfully about the ins and outs of, for example, putting up your hand. About what goes through a pupil's mind before, during and after the crazy act. Who or what told their brain it was a golden opportunity? Or told another's it was an act of self-immolation? Because it could invite ignoring or it could attract attention; it could expose a wrong or it could hail a right. Because it could lead to praise or it could render scolding; it could lead to acknowledgement, even respect, or it could lead to sarcasm, even humiliation. All this to weigh up alongside the one constant: that whatever it leads to, it is an act of publicity that you just can't retract.

Needless to say, the hand-up issue led to others. The coper, we decided, talks to their teachers and contributes in small groups; they work well alone and share successes; they take risks and join clubs; they carry equipment and turn up on time; they look after worksheets and hand in homework; they listen in class and reflect on their targets; they act on instructions and help others with learning. Let's face it, they are irritatingly perfect because they even eat and sleep well, persevere in adversity and are comfortable making mistakes.

So, we had our list. Fifty questions, including some about literacy, that each student would be asked to answer on a sliding scale of never to always, not at all to very much, or badly to very well indeed, thank you very much. (See pages 22–23.) All we needed now were our guinea pigs. Oh, and the capacity to listen.

I wonder what percentage of teacher training time, be it at university or in school, is dedicated to the art of listening. I don't just mean the hearing bit, I mean the processing bit too. What you might call listening with purpose or listening, and some. The reason I wonder is because when our new recruits first turned up in the small classroom overlooking the big field, not only did they seem to enjoy the view and the safety of a tight learning environment, but they also seemed to enjoy the opportunity to speak. In fact, the only obstacle they might face would be their teacher's inability to listen.

'Do you work well with other pupils?'

'No, I prefer working on my own.'

'OK, but do you work well when you do work with other pupils?'

'No.'

'I see. How come?'

'They don't like me.'

'All of them?'

'Pretty much.'

At that point, of course, the conversation can go one of several ways. Such as avoidance or seat-shifting. Or a lecture on friendliness and personal hygiene. Followed by more curriculum.

But the way it could go, if education allows itself and its staff the time – in the name of truly educating the self about the self – is to a deeper listening exercise, one in which the pupil is fully empowered to explain their reality of not working well with other pupils and the teacher fully disempowered to say or do anything other than to coax and listen. On a loop. With good grace. So that if only one thing comes out of that first encounter, lesson, intervention or whatever educational nomenclature you want to give it, it is that the student is able to verbalise what it feels like to feel like no one likes them. To hell with working well with other pupils, with the question on the sheet, the passport, the teacher, intervention teaching, the school. The only thing that now matters is the opportunity afforded to both speaker and listener – of both being complicit in making clear a fundamental feeling, a deeply uncomfortable feeling, that is preventing a child not just from learning but from being able, in this case, to do what ought to be the simplest of things: to make positive contact with their peers.

'Tell me what that feels like ...'

If you think that sounds like the tired retreat of the do-gooder therapist (just saying – how it sounds is how you said it), who cares? Your pupil will only know you're genuine – you will only know you're genuine – if you're prepared to engage in their world and needs. Responding with interest but dispassion, with kindness not over-sympathy, with care not faked empathy. And listening even harder when their replies interrupt your replies.

So many conversations that sprung from the passport were of this ilk:

'Do you talk to your teachers?'

'No, you must be kidding.'

'Not even sometimes?'

'No.'

'I see. How come?'

'They don't like me.'

'All of them?'

'Every one.'

'Do you put your hand up in class?'

'No.'

'How come?'

'I'm terrified.'

'Terrified of what?'

'My teacher. He hates me.'

'How do you know?'

'He shouted at me last time I answered a question.'

'When was that?'

'Six months ago.'

'Are you comfortable making mistakes?'

'No, I hate it.'

'What does it make you feel like?'

'Like I'm stupid, like everyone says.'

'Who says?'

'Everyone.'

So many insights started to emerge from these conversations. So many unspoken personal truths – truths in as much as they were true to the individual, even if not intrinsically 'true'. So much anxiety and over-worry, under-confidence and self-loathing, wariness and cynicism, so much inner turmoil and emotional pain. So much, in fact, that the initial questions started to lose their intended meaning, but not, however, their purpose: to open up the way to a healthier relationship with school. What felt like was happening was that, guards down, these pupils were starting to speak about the deeper issues behind their inability to cope with the vagaries of school and to initiate a conversation that at some stage might just yield an improvement or part-answer, even if not a full-on solution.

And from where I was sitting, and learning to listen, I could see and hear that it was a relief to us both.

CHAPTER 3

THE PASSPORT

I say *the* passport, but actually there are a few of them.[1] They sort of had children, you see. But the original, the daddy, is the literacy passport (see Figure 1). Its concept is based on the premise that to teach a struggling student literacy – so that it sticks and is meaningful – the learner needs to have other foundations in place first; or at least to be working on them at the same time. Such as a degree of confidence. A little organisation. Some positivity towards their learning. Towards you, in fact.

The passport has a front side and a back: the front (the one with the big ovals) helps pupils to identify needs; the back (the one with the rectangles) helps them to meet them. The front comprises three main sections, which I like to think of as the key areas of school – *confidence and resilience*, *organisation and presentation*, and *attitude to learning*. It also comprises a fourth section, which is particular to the subject area in which you are working, so it may be used to deal with literacy (as in the case of the literacy passport) or, more specifically, reading skills (see Figure 2 in Chapter 7), it may be about a topic in science or RE (see Figure 3 in Chapter 7), it may encompass performance in all subjects, as a means of preparation for a parents' evening (see Figure 4 in Chapter 7) or used as part of a strategy to help students reduce their long-term residence in detention (see Figure 5 in Chapter 7).

---

1   Colour copies of the passport can be downloaded for free from: https://www.crownhouse.co.uk/featured/emotional-literacy

Name: .... Date:..

CONFIDENCE AND RESILIENCE

Do I talk to teachers about my work if I don't understand it?
1 | 2 | 3

Do I contribute to small group work?
1 | 2 | 3

Am I involved in any clubs at school?
1 | 2 | 3

Do I work well with other pupils?
1 | 2 | 3

Do I share my successes with my form tutor?
1 | 2 | 3

Do I work through problems independently?
1 | 2 | 3

Do I take opportunities presented to me at school?
1 | 2 | 3

Do I put my hand up in class?
1 | 2 | 3

Do I start tasks promptly?
1 | 2 | 3

Do I find it easy to make friends?
1 | 2 | 3

LIT PAS

ORGANISATION AND PRESENTATION

Do I complete homework on time?
1 | 2 | 3

Do I look after worksheets for school?
1 | 2 | 3

Am I prepared for each lesson with the right equipment and books?
1 | 2 | 3

Do I revise for tests at school?
1 | 2 | 3

How often do I attend school?
1 | 2 | 3

Do I switch off my electronic devices an hour before going to sleep?
1 | 2 | 3

Am I on time for lessons?
1 | 2 | 3

Do I get enough sleep at night?
1 | 2 | 3

Do I dress neatly and appropriately for school?
1 | 2 | 3

Do I follow the school's presentation guidelines?
1 | 2 | 3

Do I take time to eat a good breakfast?
1 | 2 | 3

How well do I look after my planner?
1 | 2 | 3

FIGURE 1. LITERACY PASSPORT

Note: Colour copies of the passport can be downloaded for free from:
https://www.crownhouse.co.uk/featured/emotional-literacy.

Form: ....

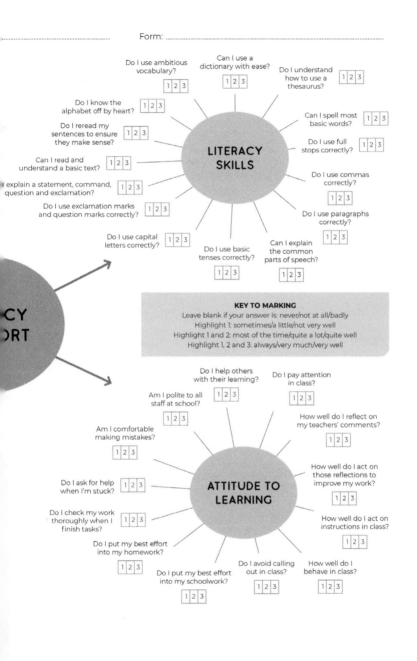

LITERACY SKILLS

Do I use ambitious vocabulary? 1 2 3

Can I use a dictionary with ease? 1 2 3

Do I understand how to use a thesaurus? 1 2 3

Do I know the alphabet off by heart? 1 2 3

Can I spell most basic words? 1 2 3

Do I reread my sentences to ensure they make sense? 1 2 3

Do I use full stops correctly? 1 2 3

Can I read and understand a basic text? 1 2 3

Do I use commas correctly? 1 2 3

explain a statement, command, question and exclamation? 1 2 3

Do I use exclamation marks and question marks correctly? 1 2 3

Do I use paragraphs correctly? 1 2 3

Do I use capital letters correctly? 1 2 3

Do I use basic tenses correctly? 1 2 3

Can I explain the common parts of speech? 1 2 3

...CY ...RT

KEY TO MARKING
Leave blank if your answer is: never/not at all/badly
Highlight 1: sometimes/a little/not very well
Highlight 1 and 2: most of the time/quite a lot/quite well
Highlight 1, 2 and 3: always/very much/very well

ATTITUDE TO LEARNING

Do I help others with their learning? 1 2 3

Do I pay attention in class? 1 2 3

Am I polite to all staff at school? 1 2 3

How well do I reflect on my teachers' comments? 1 2 3

Am I comfortable making mistakes? 1 2 3

How well do I act on those reflections to improve my work? 1 2 3

Do I ask for help when I'm stuck? 1 2 3

How well do I act on instructions in class? 1 2 3

Do I check my work thoroughly when I finish tasks? 1 2 3

Do I put my best effort into my homework? 1 2 3

Do I avoid calling out in class? 1 2 3

How well do I behave in class? 1 2 3

Do I put my best effort into my schoolwork? 1 2 3

What is my need in **confidence and resilience**?

....

What I can do to meet this need:
....
....
....

My feelings about my efforts to meet my needs:
Week 1: ....
Week 2: ....
Week 3: ....
Week 4: ....

Needs not met ○   Needs partly met ○   Needs met ○

REVIEW DATES

PUPIL

Date: ....

Date: ....

Date: ....

Date: ....

What is my need in **organisation and presentation**?

....

What I can do to meet this need:
....
....
....

My feelings about my efforts to meet my needs:
Week 1: ....
Week 2: ....
Week 3: ....
Week 4: ....

Needs not met ○   Needs partly met ○   Needs met ○

MY NEXT NEEDS

1. ....

2. ....

3. ....

4. ....

FIGURE 1. LITERACY PASSPORT

Note: Colour copies of the passport can be downloaded for free from:
https://www.crownhouse.co.uk/featured/emotional-literacy.

Whichever passport you chose to use, or to create – by inserting, in this fourth section, apt questions about the topic area you wish to teach – the concept is the same: that to help develop new skills in a specific area, such as literacy, you always underpin them by helping your student to develop key personal skills, at the same time, in the other three areas – in their *confidence and resilience*, their *organisation and presentation*, and their *attitude to learning*.

I will explain in more detail how to use these passports in Chapter 7, but, for now, I'd just like to offer you an eight-step process to follow, whichever version of the passport you choose to use.

1. SELECT YOUR PROTÉGÉ

Step 1: two minutes

Choose the student or students you'd like to let loose on this thing. They will be obvious. They're the ones screaming out for support by, well, you know how they scream for support: they throw things across classrooms; they shrug their shoulders at you; they devise exciting stories about homework malfunctions; they hold their heads below their shoulders; they blend into walls; they wear faces of assurance.

Once chosen, let your protégé know that you have an idea to share with them – a positive one – and arrange a convenient time to meet. For an hour.

What is my need in **literacy skills**?

....

What I can do to meet this need:

....

....

....

My feelings about my efforts to meet my needs:

Week 1: ....

Week 2: ....

Week 3: ....

Week 4: ....

Needs not met O   Needs partly met O   Needs met O

What is my need in **attitude to learning**?

....

What I can do to meet this need:

....

....

....

My feelings about my efforts to meet my needs:

Week 1: ....

Week 2: ....

Week 3: ....

Week 4: ....

Needs not met O   Needs partly met O   Needs met O

2. DECLARE YOUR INTEREST

Steps 2-5: 60 minutes

Be upfront from the outset: you'd like to try something with them. It's not a worksheet. And there's no homework. There are needs, however. And feelings. And lots of talking. And through a combination of all these, and lots of joint effort, you'd like to help them develop some new skills for school. And for after school, in fact. Fill in any missing info, talk them briefly through the passport, and, assuming they haven't run away or booked an Uber by now ...

3. UNLEASH THE HIGHLIGHTER (AND LISTEN)

Arm your student with their favourite weapon: the high-lighter. And explain the game. For each question they have four choices: leave the box blank, highlight just number 1, highlight numbers 1 and 2, or highlight numbers 1, 2 and 3. As per the key (on the front), their choice will depend on to what extent they feel they meet the demands of the question.

This is a good opportunity for students to self-assess. They may wish to ask questions along the way, for clarity, but do the highlighting alone, or they may wish to talk through each question with you before highlighting. Either works. I've found that the method is far less important than the deed: students spending time processing their own thoughts about their day-to-day realities at school. That said, at the end of each section of highlighting – if you haven't already – suggest talking through their answers with them. As teachers know from experience, to explain something to another is to crystallise your own understanding.

If you were to ask me for a list of dos and don'ts at this stage, it would be a short one:

Do: Listen.

Don't: Stop listening.

Initially students just want someone to hear them. Given time, and an ear, I've found that most young people are straightforwardly honest about their capacity to make friends, contribute in small groups or be on time for lessons. They seem to tackle even what you might perceive as the more personal of questions with sangfroid. Any editing that needs to take place (by redrawing and re-highlighting the boxes) will most likely come from your student.

- 'Actually, perhaps I don't always have the right equipment for lessons.'

- 'Hmm, I guess my planner could look a little less trashed.'

- 'To be honest with you, sir, I don't really reflect on my teachers' comments because I can't stand half of them – and they don't like me much either.'

As you discuss each question, listen carefully and record anything that feels important – important because it is at the heart of the blockage with the question, because it underlies the need or just because it may be important to come back to at a later stage. For example, if a student doesn't work well with others and discloses that they 'don't like it when people don't like my ideas', I would say it's worthy of note. When another lets you know that they don't take risks in lessons because 'some people laugh at me', so much so that 'I want to move form', it's also worth recording. It is not unusual to uncover bigger issues than the passport purports to handle during the highlighter step.

4. IDENTIFY NEEDS

Now that the passport has had a lick of highlighter, it's time to identify needs – rather than targets. Humour me a moment while I pit them against each other:

Target: a level or situation that you intend to achieve.

---

versus

Need: the things a person must have in order to have a satisfactory life.[2]

While the questions on this passport are all things 'you intend to achieve' – such as making friends and getting enough sleep – it would seem to me that many are also requirements of 'a satisfactory life'; something any pupil should reasonably expect.

Assuming we want pupils to have a decent life, in and out of school, we should start thinking about their school

---

2   According to the Cambridge Dictionary online: https://dictionary.cambridge.org/dictionary/english/need.

experience in terms of needs rather than targets – hence the switch of terminology here (although don't be surprised when the 't' word continues to slip out).

By now, each section on the front will likely have several boxes with just 1s, or indeed nothing, highlighted. Ask your pupil to reread these questions and, for each section, choose which question they would most like to work on for the next four weeks. It's really important that they're not led on this – the more they want a need to be met, the more likely it is they will commit to doing what's necessary to meet it. Should they want help in deciding, a few pertinent questions from you should help confirm. Once established, ask them to circle it.

At the end of this exercise, you should have four questions circled, ready to transfer to the back of the sheet. Using the wording in the chosen questions, flip the passport over and ask the pupil to write in their needs for each section – for example 'To work well with other pupils' or 'To complete homework on time'. Don't let them shortcut this part, otherwise you'll end up with contracted sentences like 'other pupils', 'homework!!!', 'go to school 😟' and 'be polite 😠'. All of which are great pointers, but in their vagueness are also great for slipping out of – an art form cleverly invented by pupil-kind.

5. WORK OUT THE HOW

One section at a time, you now need to tackle the hardest part of the passport together, the *how* – known, in this case, as 'What I can do to meet this need'. I've approached this section in a variety of different ways. The least spectacular involved equipping children with a crib sheet, which suggested possible ways to tackle the different needs. In my head, they would use them to spark their own ideas; in their heads, I'd just given them the 'answers'.

The best way for this section to be done well is to talk it through – or as far through as you can take it. Clearly, a young person who isn't finding it easy to make friends isn't going to suddenly find their inner socialite with the first few ill-chosen ideas that come into their head – like 'just chat to everyone' or 'make new friends, stupid'. Given free rein, your pupil will content themselves with the first solution that comes to mind, so it's vital that both of you understand that you're not just 'filling in a section' here. In reality, you're giving your pupil an opportunity to re-educate themselves on why they are how they are, and what it might take from them to change this for the better. No mean feat, but it can be done, starting with good questioning and an environment of openness.

Whether your pupil's chosen needs involve issues of confidence, organisation or attitude, there will likely be a whole myriad of reasons why the highlighter ink has been economised on these issues. So dig deep.

'Tell me, what does it feel like putting your hand up in class? What goes through your mind? What do you think is going to happen? What happens normally, physically as well as emotionally? What happens when you are chosen to answer, regardless of your hand going up? Are the feelings similar to any other experience you have in life? How do you deal with that?

'Is there a way of making it less difficult? Can I share with you what it felt like for me when I was a child? Are there teachers with whom you feel more comfortable putting your hand up? Is there one lesson in which you could aim to put your hand up once a week? Or even once a day? Would you prefer to start with writing answers down on a piece of paper to show your teachers at the end? Would you be happy to ask them if they're OK with that?'

If you're thinking that's a bit intense, you might want to let them answer in the middle. Joking aside though, I realise none of us are trained therapists, but it sometimes takes an awful lot of questions – bearing in mind that the answers will at first be quite half-baked and a tad evasive – to start to unpick a need. This is highly personal stuff and is not territory in which any of us is particularly comfortable yet. However, and I can only speak from my own experience here, these *are* conversations that young people are itching to have. So have them, and only when you feel you have drilled down to the nub of each issue, and through your conversation helped to persuade your pupil that they themselves can positively impact their own need, only then should you invite them to record the ideas you've arrived at together in the 'What I can do to meet this need' section.

However, your work for this section is not yet quite done. In order to ensure that your time has been well spent and that these needs are firmly on not just your pupil's but all relevant parties' agendas, you need to type them up (from the 'What is my need in …?' section) and print them out. On nice, bright stickers. Twice. One set can go at the front of their planner and one set in their exercise book. Needs have been established, together with plans, and now everyone who wants to be – whether your pupil's parents, carers, teaching assistant, learning support assistant, form tutor or head of year – can be in on them.

Should any needs feel too sensitive to be detailed in these places, agree they need not be typed up and printed.

Step 5 complete, politely suggest you look after the passport for safekeeping. Beyond that, assuming a jumping high five feels premature, quietly arrange a new time to meet in order that you can ...

6. RECORD FEELINGS AND IMPACT

Step 6: 30 minutes each week for four weeks

A week has gone by. You meet as arranged, exchanging pleasantries while hunting around for wherever you left that damn passport. You sit down and look your student in the eye. A slightly unsure eye it is. You remind them about the reason for your meeting, asking them to read back to you their first need and how they were going to start to meet that need. They stumble over what they wrote, some of it illegible. And as they do, you get that dreaded fear that your previous conversation – the one you both worked so hard to make happen, on a level you had not talked on before and had made so much sense at the time – has somehow become vinegar-soaked chip paper: ditched without a second thought and idling away somewhere in the dustbin of school time.

A week is a long time at school. You can ask a student about what happened in your lesson yesterday and they can look at you like they're not even sure who you are. Whole lifetimes seem to pass in one day sometimes. Students come in broadly kempt and ready, if not raring, to go. And then you see them later and they're shadows of their former, this morning, selves: bag's been lost, eyes have gone, they're laughing like a maniac and their body's turned to jelly; they've picked up umpteen warnings, a brace of detentions; pen streaks their arms, mud cakes their shoes; they've got their best mate's head in an arm-lock and they're swaying down the corridor, inebriated by the fumes of school rule and ritual, conduct and conformity. So much to take in, take on, take out on someone, so much unwanted stuff that very little remains – very little in terms of education – to make them whole again.

But your fears are unfounded because, actually, despite the initial eyes and demeanour, having read through their first need and their first 'how to', your student does indeed remember your conversation. And what it is they were supposed to do on behalf of themselves. And despite all the carnage that had filled the space in-between, in that light year of a week at school, they look at you as if to say, 'You know what, that did actually mean something to me. It was a conversation for me, about me, in the interests of, and trying to help, me. And, even though I'd totally forgotten what I promised to do, I do remember and recognise this form of learning. I might even quite like it.'

'So, Kieran, how did you get on asking your form tutor on what days of the week football club runs?'

'Er, well, I did mean to ... but then I forgot, sir.'

'OK, does that mean you also forgot to ask if any of your mates want to join too?'

'Er, yes.'

'And if you can get a lift?'

'Yes, that too.'

'OK, and I guess that also means you've not gone to any sessions?'

'Yeah.'

'No problem. Thanks for your honesty. How are we going to sort it? What will help you remember?'

'Don't know, sir.'

'How about a reminder in your planner, so that when your teacher asks you to open it during registration, it will jump out at you and remind you to ask?'

'Yeah, I can do that.'

'Good. Please do. Right now.'

Writes.

'So how do you feel about your efforts to meet this need this week, Kieran?'

'Er, not too clever. I think I could have done a bit better.'

'That seems honest. Why not write it down ...'

The 'My feelings about my efforts to meet my needs' section is there to capture introspection. And good, honest self-analysis being the slippery eel that it is, this is also an area of the passport that needs time, as well as open, non-judgemental questioning. After all, you're both on the same side – you've invested in a process that deigns to improve a behaviour in one of you. You criticising non-effort in that person can quite easily lead to no effort. Them observing their own non-effort, or effort with a degree of failure, or effort with a degree of success, can help lead to education – your student's, about the reality of their endeavours.

So when you hear it, applaud their honesty. Because, as Bangalorean author Pratheek Praveen Kumar explains in his book *My Time, My World*, 'honesty breeds confidence and nourishes self-respect. It makes us upright and honourable'.[3] A point which author and researcher Courtney E. Ackerman develops, saying that self-esteem, in turn, 'provides us with belief in our abilities and the

---

3   P. P. Kumar, *My Time, My World* (Kindle Edition, 2009), p. 105

motivation to carry them out, ultimately reaching fulfillment as we navigate life with a positive outlook'.[4]

Each week, record feelings about efforts to meet needs, regardless of whether they involve being 'so proud' or 'so disappointed' or so somewhere in-between. At the same time, record impact. The passport is a working document so don't you, or your student, be afraid to scribble all over it, dotted line or not, capturing relevant anecdotes and insights which help to tell the story of one student's efforts to meet one student's needs. Impact at school, impact at home, impact on friendship, impact on confidence, whatever you deem pertinent. And when you've done that, go back to feelings and discuss how it feels to have done something that has had a positive (or, thus far, negative) impact on something that wasn't previously working. And invite your student to own the success (or, thus far, lack of it) by writing it down. Anywhere they want. Yes, you may end up with a car crash of scribbled notes veering this way and that, but ultimately it will be a collision of ink that you'll both reflect over with some satisfaction and pride.

Last thing on this one: to conclude your weekly proceedings, date and sign accordingly in the box provided.

7. MAKE THE CALL

Steps 7–8: 30 minutes

At the end of week 4's reflections, your student is asked to make a judgement. As with the questions, it could be one they initially arrive at on their own or that you arrive at together. Either way, it is one that necessitates a short

---

4   C. E. Ackerman, What is self-esteem? A psychologist explains, *Positive Psychology* (16 April 2020). Available at https://positivepsychology.com/self-esteem.

period of discussion and looking back over. Naturally, there is a tendency for both parties to want to tick the 'needs met' box, and that is the most important thing to remember when overseeing this stage. Indeed, whether a need has been met, partially met or not met is not, to my mind, paramount. After all, a met need could yet have a fall to come, or a still unmet need could have all the right measures in place to be met in due course. To me, the key is the process. It is the thorough completion of the passport process that will start to yield the emotional literacy necessary to continue to tackle not just this but many a future need. So, if you suspect a slightly generous assessment of the situation by either one of you, rein it in. At this stage, it's better to call it how it is or, if in doubt, to understate; Rome wasn't built in a month.

8. DECIDE WHAT'S NEXT

The last thing that remains, for this passport at least, is for your student to fill in the 'my next needs' box. It is advisable for them to keep any existing needs which remain 'not met' or 'partly met' in this list – continued work on a particular area calls for determination, which in turn will help to develop resilience. To complete the list, turn to the front of the passport, re-discuss questions that attracted a lack of highlighter four weeks ago, and ask your student to select their next priorities – by which time, you will have completed one round of the passport.

How long you can continue passport work with a particular student, beyond this first round, will depend on the usual school variables of time, money and priorities. None of them are invalid but let me finish by observing that the more practice you both get at this, the better you'll both get. And, of course, once a rapport has developed between you, the more potent and rewarding your collaborations will become.

THE POLITICS OF INTRUSION

It won't be lost on you that some questions the passport asks of its filler-inner are close to the mark. They threaten to cross the line between a school's business and a pupil's – indeed, a pupil's family's business. I'm thinking in particular of questions of breakfast and sleep. Both have the potential to create embarrassment or humiliation for parents, carers and young people. And, of course, the last thing you want is for them to believe that you are judging their parenting skills or, in the pupil's case, the skills of their parents.

There is a danger of this happening, regardless of how you handle it. However, my feeling is that the importance of the issues outweighs the risks of tackling them. The parts played by food and sleep in a pupil's day need no exaggeration.

According to the conclusions of one study of 9- to 11-year-olds, led by Cardiff University research associate Hannah J. Littlecott, 'Significant positive associations between … breakfast consumption and educational outcomes were observed.' Indeed, it was also suggested that communicating the educational benefits of breakfast to schools 'may help to enhance buy-in to efforts to improve health behaviours of pupils'.[5]

---

5 H. J. Littlecott, G. F. Moore, L. Moore and R. A. Lyons, Association between breakfast consumption and educational outcomes in 9-11-year-old children, *Public Health Nutrition*, 19(9) (2016): 1575–1582. Available at: https://pubmed.ncbi.nlm.nih.gov/26411331.

As for sleep, it is clear to lecturer in psychology Jakke Tamminen that it is 'a central part of learning'. As he says: 'Even though you're not studying when you sleep, your brain is still studying. It's almost like it's working on your behalf. You can't really get the full impact of the time you put into your studies unless you sleep.'[5]

So, if you can, have the conversations about breakfast and sleep, and do so with openness and by listening. Just like with so many of the other questions, the reasons for neglecting these two areas are generally much more about organisation, habit and pace of life – let's face it, who doesn't struggle to breakfast and sleep well sometimes? – than they are about neglect.

HOW TO USE THE PASSPORT: A SUMMARY

1 Select your protégé: choose a student who you know is struggling at school, let them know you have an idea to share, and arrange a time to meet.

2 Declare your interest: tell them you'd like to help. Talk them through the passport and let them know you're primarily going to be listening to their feelings and needs.

3 Unleash the highlighter (and listen): ask your student to highlight the boxes on the front, while

---

6 Quoted by C. Ro, Why sleep should be every student's priority, *BBC Future* (20 August 2018). Available at: https://www.bbc.com/future/article/20180815-why-sleep-should-be-every-students-priority

listening to their thoughts about each question and noting down anything that strikes you as key.

4   Identify needs: ask your student to choose, as their needs, one question from each section and circle it. Have them copy each one out in the space given on the reverse of the passport.

5   Work out the how: talk through each need in detail and come up with joint suggestions about what your student can do to help meet them. Type up and print out the needs to stick in planners and exercise books.

6   Record feelings and impact: encourage sharing of feelings about efforts to meet needs. Applaud honesty and record impact and insights before dating and signing.

7   Make the call: have a discussion with your student to help decide if their needs are, thus far, 'not met', 'partly met' or 'met'. Err on the side of caution if in doubt.

8   Decide what's next: retain any existing needs that have not yet been met, before returning to the front of the passport to discuss what else your student deems 'my next needs' to complete said box.

CHAPTER 4

BEHIND THE QUESTIONS: CONFIDENCE AND RESILIENCE

Think about the most confident pupil you know. Not just superficially confident but, to the extent that any sub-16 person-in-the-making can be, beneath the surface too. Think about what they do – not just what they do that is a demonstration or effect of that confidence, but also what they do that sustains it. Acknowledge, of course, that a raft of crafting and nurture, much of it initiated outside school, of genes and world experience are likely behind that sure-footed confidence. But then think also about how even a small but potent drop of that confidence could look on some of your less confident pupils.

It is in this part-dream state that it is worth approaching the *confidence and resilience* section. The passport offers ten questions that feel very much linked with these swashbuckling attributes, but they are by no means comprehensive or the result of a long scientific study. They are just what came from the result of the thinking exercise above. In this section, I will describe each question to different degrees of depth. Your own passport may keep some, all or none of these. What matters is what works: the hallmarks of this section in your place of education and with your pupils.

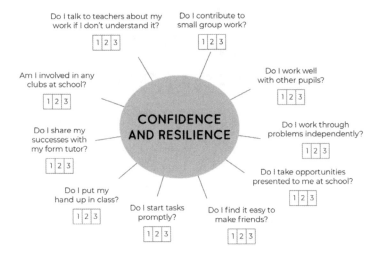

DO I TALK TO TEACHERS ABOUT MY WORK IF I DON'T UNDERSTAND IT?

I always start at five to eleven for some reason on the circle of questions, but you can start wherever you like, obviously.

Educational staff know that pupils, and indeed parents, who put themselves on their teacher's agenda get more attention. A quick hand up during the lesson, a word before, several after or a quick chat in the corridor has the dual effect of supporting a pupil's learning *and* alerting a teacher to the needs and sometimes even presence of a particular pupil. Just like when a parent makes contact with a staff member, whether by email, phone or at a parents' evening. And in the case of both, it indicates a level of self-confidence to tackle a matter of school head-on.

Pupils who have highlighted 1 (or nothing) on this question know that it's not their thing. But in time, perhaps it can be. Approaching someone like your teacher can obviously be a daunting prospect for someone who rarely or never has, so small steps are clearly needed here. For those with greet-at-the-door teachers (love those, just saying) maybe the pupil can start by simply saying hello, ideally with head raised but any version will do. A week of that is a week well spent. Next time – only when no other child is in a ten-mile radius, of course – maybe even a 'Thank you' on the way out. Another week of that, another week well spent. From there, who knows.

Reading your pupil's cringe-ometer will tell you how far they can be pushed. Some will make a leap to then engaging their teacher about work; others won't. In which case, another stepping stone will need to be put in place. Plan it out with them: what are they comfortable doing? If very little else, who could they enlist for help? Maybe they could ask you to ask their teacher to be aware that they would like to talk to them about their work – they've still done something constructive, however vicariously, to try to effect a change. As with all the other passport questions, so long as they see that their actions are having an effect on the changing dynamic between them and their situation, then perhaps a once quite fixed mindset can edge towards growth.[1] It maybe goes without saying but I'd suggest one teacher, one subject at a time.

---

1   For more on mindset see Carol Dweck's *Mindset: How You Can Fulfil Your Potential* (London: Constable & Robinson, 2012).

MILENA[2]

What is my need in confidence and resilience?

'Talk to teachers about my work if I don't understand it.'

What I can do to meet this need:

'Speak to my English teacher once a weak for something that I don't know. When she goes to help someone else catch her eye to come over so hopefuly she doesn't call my name.'

My feelings about my efforts to meet my needs:

Week 1: 'Not yet because I feel like I don't have the confidence to do it.'

Week 2: 'I felt proud of myself to do something I wouldn't normaly do.'

Week 3: 'I feel proud of myself talking to my English teacher about [the position of] my seat. I have also talked to her about poetry and I feel good about that.'

Week 4: 'I am pleased with myself and feel like I can do more things if I set my mind to it.'

Needs partly met ✓

---

2   All student comments have been reproduced verbatim.

DO I CONTRIBUTE TO SMALL GROUP WORK?

There are ways, and there are ways, of contributing to small groups. There's the all-consuming Scout leader who bosses the joint, not letting anyone get a word in edgeways and issuing instructions like they're the Second Coming, just with less grace – we can certainly say they've contributed. There's the second-in-command contributor, echoing the words and instructions of the unelected leader, there to get the second-best roles and careful not to ally themselves too closely with the hoi polloi – they also contribute, no question. There are the shy contributors who assert their ideas but not their personalities, so are less likely to be heard – they certainly try to contribute. And there are the shy non-contributors, who assert nothing on anyone, at most paying partial attention to a party to which they're obviously not invited – they have clearly not contributed.

No doubt the Association of Small Group Workers would be able to provide a more exhaustive list, but the point is that there would appear to be different ways of contributing to a small group, plenty of which are really quite unwelcome. If adults can make a thorough hash of such interactions – and none of us needed to watch *The Office* to know that this could be so – then our offspring are certainly capable of doing so too. To tackle this question, emotionally intelligent conversation is key.

Perhaps the question should really read: 'Do you contribute to small group work even when there are generally several shades of carnage breaking out in your small groups, initiated by several autocrats in the making, the instructions for which weren't that clear and no one gives a toss what you think anyway?' In which case, a lack of highlighter might seem reasonable. I guess the message here is that you can't control others' actions, but you can control your own.

'If you have an idea, do you suggest it? Are you more likely to let others do the suggesting, assuming the role of con-scientious non-partaker? Do you get forgotten? Has your lack of previous engagement typecast you as a redundant force? Do you not really like people that much and would rather not have to work with them? In short, are groups not your bag?'

Whatever the answers, they are the building blocks for any next steps.

'You'd like to improve this scenario, it's your chosen need, so what would you like to do to affect it? What one thing could you do differently next time you're in a group? Even before then, is there anything you could do to feel more confident next time around? Befriend someone in class? Contribute more to the main lesson? Keep up with home-work so the group work in the lesson makes more sense? Give yourself a target of one contribution to one small group per week?'

If the issue seems much deeper than this, a distinct social or mental block, then it behoves the both of you to look at this first – in whatever way you feel comfortable. For me, a spot of family bashing never goes amiss: 'My wife doesn't like people much either; they get on her nerves. She says she'd be fine working with people if they would just shut up and let her sort it out. She says the same to me. You'd like her.' Which sometimes paves the way for the bones of what you'd really like to say:

'Would you like to feel more comfortable with other peo-ple? Is there anything you can think that the school could offer that would help with that? Like a club or a counsellor or maybe a mentor? Do you know what they do? You could always ask me to find out about one for you, if you do ...'

You may suddenly be a long way from working in small groups, but somehow that doesn't seem to matter any-more – something much more important might be underway.

JORDAN

What is my need in confidence and resilience?

'Contribute to smal group.'

What I can do to meet this need:

'Find a group I feel confodent in and contribut my ideas. Ignore people who are unkind.'

[Teacher note: Student says he feels like he's 'not needed' and that other groups are 'perfect and don't need me'.]

My feelings about my efforts to meet my needs:

Week 1: 'I feel good about contributing my ideas.'

Week 2: 'I enjoyed contributing again and some peo-ple listened.'

Week 3: 'No need to contribut my ideas.'

Week 4: 'Feel good for contributing in drama and peo-ple doing my ideas.'

Needs partly met ✓

DO I WORK WELL WITH OTHER PUPILS?

Clearly, this question overlaps considerably with the previous one. Find out what lies at the heart of this non-working-well. Are there underlying issues of bullying or withdrawal? Have you detected a personality trait that might be stopping the social process? Tease it out because if they trust you, they will tell you more than you need to know in order to help with the what-next.

DO I WORK THROUGH PROBLEMS INDEPENDENTLY?

Solving your own problems is a learned art – and one that is not always well learned. Take it from someone who avoids having to deal with letters by just not opening them. Or emails. Or answering phone calls. I'd almost rather take the fine than fill in the form. In school terms, though, this question of independent problem-solving could mean anything from pupils working alone to understand something they've not initially grasped – using resilience to find a way through confusion – to issues of organisation. Whatever the area of school life, the question is, in short, 'Do I sort my own shit out?' Though perhaps leave them to summarise as such.

I guess confidence to do the faecal deed comes from trying, and trying comes from daring, and daring comes from, well, where does daring coming from? A good dose of nature, a smattering of nurture, a sudden rush of blood, a moment of bloody-mindedness, some tactful encouragement. They're all candidates, but this last one in particular is where you obviously come in. Before doing the actual encouragement, the crucial I-believe-in-you stuff, it's important to dig for examples because despite being determined to espouse total self-doubt, off-guard your pupil will likely reveal something of how they've previously resolved a problem alone, however small. And it's this, or these, nuggets of evidence that are the platform on which you will build your case for further self-resolution.

'Got you! You have worked through your own problems. I knew you must have. What was different? How were the ingredients of that situation different from most you encounter? How can we apply your abilities in the successful situation to the one in which you struggle? Any ideas? Tell you what, scribble some down, I'll do the same, and we'll give the best ones a try.'

DO I TAKE OPPORTUNITIES PRESENTED TO ME AT SCHOOL?

'What does that mean, sir?'

It's a telling question because those who do will likely know instinctively that they do. Opportunities come in all shapes and sizes at school. The opportunity to hand out books in class, to take a paper register to reception, to wipe the board, to answer a question, to pick up the bin that someone else knocked over before scarpering. And then there are the opportunity opportunities – to run for the school council, to take parents on school tours, to sign up for the school choir or orchestra, to join the rugby, football, chess or superhuman-maths-problem-solving team, to redesign the school logo – the opportunity to be the best damned student this school has ever seen and to have it recognised in elegant lettering, writ large at the front of the school hall: 'Adele Chambers, Head Girl, 2019–2020'.

In answer to your pupil's question about the passport question – a very wide-ranging one, on reflection – you might respond: 'Do you do stuff that comes up or avoid it like the plague? What's your mode of operation: serial opportunity-taker, shunner or somewhere in-between?' It would be convenient to think that there's a character profile for such a type, but actually, if school teaches us anything, it's that there's really no telling. When a semi-literate pupil, barely a read book to their name, their alphabet still a-jumble, their speech but half-decodable, nearly knocks their desk over volunteering to lead open evening tours, you realise you know nothing; that taking opportunities is a mixture of so many different things that we need to treat young people very much on their own merit.

In keeping with the general ethos of the passport, I've found that to start small and build is not a bad place to kick off, so probe for the small opportunities your pupil might like to begin with. Show them that even a pile of books collected, just once in a week, is an opportunity to show willing, responsibility and general good-heartedness; to get your face in the picture, to show you count and are there to be counted. And if the book-collecting is too scary or public, then go for less. You might even have an opportunity to offer them yourself, if only someone could prompt them to ask.

REECE

What is my need in confidence and resilience?

'To take opportunities presented to me at school.'

What I can do to meet this need:

'Approach members of staff for opportunities, listen out for opportunities during form time and in assembly. Go for things I enjoy.'

My feelings about my efforts to meet my needs:

Week 1: 'I spoke to my art teacher to go on an art trip.'

Week 2: 'I took a medical course. I felt neutral.'

Week 3: 'I have listened out, nothing so far.'

Week 4: 'Took the option to go to belgium and learn more about trench warfare.'

[Teacher note: Student says he feels more confident to 'speak up and take opportunities'.]

Needs met ✓

DO I FIND IT EASY TO MAKE FRIENDS?

Does anyone? I imagine some do, but you would think that most people's honest answer to this question would be a resounding, 'No – it's bloody hard work.' But many of us persevere and do it, to differing degrees, because we realise innately that to share our lives with others (whom we like and by whom we are liked) is somehow to feel more human. For many of us, school and pre-school is the beginning of our friendship-making journey – our first foray into the social jungle.

Schools are, by implication, social places, with all manner of friendships being established, challenged, enjoyed, regretted, ridiculed and broken in pretty much equal measure every day. In fact, were they to have no academically educational properties of which to boast, you could argue that schools would still be worth their weight in whiteboard ink as social networks for young people: there to hone your friend-making basics – you know, that Mia isn't necessarily a good friend just because she comes to talk at you every day, pausing neither for breath nor answer; and that Bradley, always humiliating you in front of your other mates but being friendly one-to-one, isn't the best of platforms for future play dates. The basics, in fact, on which the rest of your child and adult life will be based.

At the heart of this question, therefore, is your pupil's view of themselves as a social and befriendable being. Do they even see themselves as someone who is worth being a friend with? Someone with qualities worth sharing, who at the same time can appreciate similar qualities in someone else? And not only do they have the capacity or self-esteem to be a friend to someone, but do they even want to be theirs or anyone else's mate?

Yes, these are all questions very much beyond the usual school realm, but why is that? If the bedrock of school is being social, and good social skills are widely linked with higher achievement – according to a meta-analysis of school-based learning programmes involving over 250,000 young people, students who received social skills instruction, compared to control groups, 'demonstrated significantly improved social and emotional skills, attitudes, behaviour and academic performance that reflected an 11-percentile-point gain in achievement'[3] – should they not have as equal a footing as any other questions of learning or discussion at

---

3   J. A. Durlak, R. P. Weissberg, A. B. Dymnicki, R. B. Taylor and K. B. Schellinger, The impact of enhancing students' social and emotional learning: a meta-analysis of school-based universal interventions, *Child Development*, 82(1) (2011): 405–432 at 405. Available at: http://www.casel.org/wp-content/uploads/2016/01/meta-analysis-child-development-1.pdf.

school? Equal footing with, say, three weeks on Pythagoras, a day of pyramidal peaks, a short-term plan of punctuation (however wonderfully embedded)? None of them un-important – particularly for those aspiring to one day have jobs in triangles or mountain-part identification – but are they that much superior to the deeper questions of friendship?

I would argue not. So, have the conversation, unpick the need and ferret for solutions. It's surprising how much emotional self-knowledge pupils possess in the deeper reaches of their unconscious minds. One boy reflected, not long after completely annihilating himself to me as a friend-making specimen, in not so few words but with considerable aplomb, that in order to make better friends he just needed to: 'Think twice before doing something dumb. Make eye contact. Listen before I speak. Be myself – not someone I'm trying to be.'

DO I START TASKS PROMPTLY?

The beauty of this question lies in its dual purpose: to improve the speed with which one attends to a particular instruction or assignment in a scholastic setting and to learn a new word.

'What does "promptly" mean, sir?'

'It means as quickly as you asked me that follow-up question.'

'Oh.'

From a teacher's-eye view, confident pupils start tasks pretty much the second they've been asked. That is not to say that they necessarily pick up a pen and start writing, or a ball and start practising, but they start attending to the task with which they've been, well, tasked. And, as we all know, that can look like many different things. It can look like quiet thinking or thinking aloud; it can look like standing up, collecting something or moving to a place of learning; it can look like a hand up with a question; it can even look like a rebuke to a neighbour to please kindly refrain from their relentless waffle.

What it doesn't look like, of course, is a paper aeroplane across the classroom. Or a head on the table. Or on the back of the chair, mouth agape and whining, with its body spread generously across, in front and to the side of, the seat. It also doesn't look like a snapped pencil, a furiously vibrating ruler or a tactical change of conversation. And it doesn't look like the deathly silence which greets you when you've explained something so badly that even your teaching assistant is looking around them like they've temporarily forgotten who they are. Regardless of its cause, if anyone knows what starting a task promptly doesn't look like, it's the teacher.

And as, by and large, the creator of said delays, it's also the pupil. So, if your one has chosen this one as their need in this section, then push them to reflect on (a) how they delay getting started with tasks and, more importantly, (b) why. The first part may go on for some while and with some hilarity – you could write a short book on the range of techniques, some more ingenious than others – but hear it out because it's part of the cleansing that should pave the way for the second.

Were I part of a betting syndicate taking money on the most popular answers to (b), I'd argue my case for the following odds:

2/1: I never understand the work.

5/2: I don't know how to get started.

4/1: I never understand/listen to the instructions.

9/2: I can't concentrate for long enough to understand the instructions.

5/1: My teachers are all boring.

7/1: What's the point in school anyway?

10/1: My pen broke so I had to put it back together again, and the spring kept popping out just before I'd fixed it, so the lesson ended before I could even get started.

12/1: My cat died.

'Yes, and what about the other times you lack promptness to start?'

'It happens a lot, sir.'

As passport officiator, it's your job to sift through the answers, giving credence and airtime where warranted. But even beneath what we might think of as the more creative, less virtuous answers, there will inevitably be an underlying reason (or reasons) why this particular child is not champing at the bit to start tasks in lessons. Explore concentration and comprehension, among other markers, and see what chimes most with your pupil. It might be that all they need in each lesson is a quick chat with a fellow pupil or teaching assistant to check their understanding; they may need a quiet minute with the teacher once the initial explanation is complete; they may need more differentiated tasks or less distracting neighbours; they may need their own abilities to concentrate looked into – there is help out there, which they could be prompted to ask you to investigate, should you agree that it seems to be warranted.

Whatever your (plural, always plural) findings, they are the precursor to your pupil writing down ways that they can positively influence their self-diagnosed inability or reluctance to start tasks promptly. And when you ask them to do so, you might find yourselves sharing a wry smile if it doesn't happen altogether immediately.

AMRITA

What is my need in confidence and resilience?

'To start tasks promptly.'

What I can do to meet this need:

'To ask my form tutor to remind me to keep this up in every lesson. Stop delaying by talking to my friends. Get to lessons on time.'

My feelings about my efforts to meet my needs:

Week 1: 'My teachers have noticed my improvement.'

Week 2: 'Remind form tutor to remind me on Wednesday.'

Week 3: 'Started well and carried on. Happy.'

Week 4: 'Went back a little over Christmas but did it well and better this week. I am proud.'

Needs partly met ✓

DO I PUT MY HAND UP IN CLASS?

How many ways can you think of that children put their hands up? There's the fully standing, chair gone for a burton, arm being pulled out of its socket by the opposing arm's hand, ooh sounds, ignore me and I'll trash the classroom and never answer another question for you again hand up; there's the no-nonsense, quick-as-a-flash hand to the sky, face a picture of assured knowledge hand up; there's the sideways-leaning, tired, wonky, neighbour-invading hand up; there's the nervous, elbow attached to hip, one finger, I think I know the answer and I'd like you to know that I think I might know the answer, but for goodness' sake don't pick me hand up; there's even the double-armed howzat plus full-on waving hands up, but thankfully it's a rarer sight once the less self-conscious days of primary are over.

All those ways, and plenty more, of putting your hand up and, for some reason, we've still got pupils tucking them under their hamstrings, burying them in their armpits, clutching one with another or just stoically keeping them anywhere other than above resting level. So why is that? As touched on in Chapter 2, there are as many reasons why someone might not put their hand up as there are ways of so doing, so if your pupil chooses this as their confidence and resilience need, it's one that will likely – and rightly – take time to investigate.

I can remember – the feeling more than the event – when I first put my hand up as a practising journalist. I was at a press conference, right at the back, maybe a hundred people in the room, and as the speaker finished I inched up my hand. I've no idea what I asked, or what was answered, but I knew I had to ask the question, if only to get me off the mark in my new profession. The thing that stuck with me, apart from the rush of relief, was the feeling of voicing something (albeit nervously) in public and being heard and responded to with respect – it was like being sprinkled with a type of confidence-inducing fairy dust. I walked out of the room two inches taller.

It would seem to be generally true that you get the confidence to do more of something the more you do it, but also that you lose the confidence to do any amount of something the less you do it. Aside from avoiding the latter, the million dollar question is, how on earth do you get started on the former?

Had that first press conference question gone unspeakably wrong, or even just wrong, I would no doubt have thought twice about asking my second, which would likely have delayed the third and made less likely a fourth. And that in the case of a moderately confident, moderately assured adult. Pupils, often neither of those things, can carry their negative hand-up experiences around with them like stains across the heart, which, it would seem, unshared and unexplored, can dictate this one aspect of their classroom etiquette for the whole of their education.

While being mindful of the impact of their words and tone to any one child, it's clear that teaching staff can't be wholly responsible for every child's feelings, every time they respond to an answer in class. Every single teacher will get this wrong – a misjudged joke, an over-reaction to an error, a poorly judged sarcastic quip. And that's partly because the pupils themselves are in a constant flux of getting stuff (not just answers) wrong, which the teacher may themselves be reacting to, and partly because to err is human – whether you're the responsible adult or otherwise. That's not to excuse teaching staff who make a habit, knowingly or otherwise, of denigrating or humiliating children; too many pupils, past and present, bear the scars to know that is a dereliction of duty.

Notwithstanding these exceptions, which should clearly be dealt with on a professional level, the important detail for your pupil is that they can only control *their* aspect of this situation. But in so doing, they may also come to see that they can also have influence on their teacher, so that they notice them and can see that they're willing, that they want to take part and learn.

Where appropriate, talk through when their last answer earned no more than short shrift; or when the teacher, and then the whole class, laughed; when their cheeks burned with shame, the donkey noises reverberating well beyond 3.20pm; when they last put their hand up because the experience was so miserable it certainly wouldn't be happening again very soon, if ever. Listen, show empathy, share stories, and at the end of this session, or maybe next, start over.

How? As mentioned in Chapter 3, in the 'Work out the how' section, by coming up with the small things that might start to turn around this learned inability. One hand up a week with a preferred teacher even to ask, not answer, a question, is a step on the road to renewed confidence and resilience.

KYRA

What is my need in confidence and resilience?

'To put my hand up in class.'

What I can do to meet this need:

'Put my hand up once a lesson in maths. Think of the past to overcome my fears. Remember it is OK to make mistakes.'

My feelings about my efforts to meet my needs:

Week 1: 'Was brave and got the answer correct.'

Week 2: 'Proud that I pushed myself to answer questions again.'

Week 3: 'Pleased that I achieved something twice that I find difficult.'

Week 4: 'Pleased I pushed myself to do something I'm not comfortable with three times in maths. Feel like I need to put my hand up more in English and other classes now.'

Needs partly met ✓

DO I SHARE MY SUCCESSES WITH MY FORM TUTOR?

'Do I what?'

This question falls into a category of what you might call deliberately presupposing: firstly, that everyone has successes; secondly, that they would want to share them; and, thirdly, that they would want to do so with their form tutor.

'Why would I want to do that?'

I've answered this question a number of times, but never to any degree with which I've been really happy. I guess I'm struggling to convey a belief that to notice and then to share what you do well is to start to embed it in your life. And from which you can take confidence. See, I still can't do it.

The point is that pupils who do well generally know what they do well. And the more precocious among them won't stop letting you know not just what they've done well but, all in all, just how bloody marvellous they are. That's not what I'm advocating here. I'm advocating that the scales are balanced out a little, so that for every assertion of 'Whoa, get me' and 'I'm the greatest' we hear in school, we're also picking up a few whispers along the lines of, 'I feel a little bit proud of what I did there, miss.'

Success, like beauty, is in the eye of the beholder. Helping your younger brother to release anger by reading to him is only a success if you compare it to what happens when he's left alone; reading out loud in class when you're terrified and dyslexic is only a success when you realise the size of the hurdle you've just overcome; making a ninetieth-minute tackle that stopped a goal and meant that Charlie Big Potaters could go down the other end and equalise – and take all of the applause – is only a success if you see that without it, you'd have lost.

The language of school and success is largely broached in distinct and wholly biased terms: getting good marks and winning. That's my list. So much of what we do at school, and what is seen as successful, is about grade-getting and competition-winning. Even when schools are mindfully aware of this, going out of their way to acknowledge effort and hard work, they still sometimes seem to find a way to have winners and, by implication, losers – or pupils gaining pass marks or failure ones. Even if it's not said in these terms, it's what we, and more importantly they, understand.

Winning, losing, passing and failing are all parts of life. In themselves, there's nothing wrong with young people finding them out at school, and, indeed, learning that to appreciate one you sometimes need to have experienced the other. My point is not that we need to ban winning and losing – far from it, they are vital parts of growing up; it's that we need to broaden our categories of what success looks like. If we acknowledge that we're all different, that we each have different skills, at different stages of development, we ought also to acknowledge that success

– and the celebration of it – should be a much more varied thing too.

So, yes, if your pupil has dug deep to deal well with a bully, then that is a magnificent success – of resilience and emotional control. No award necessary – just important to know that they did something well and that it is deeply respected. And if they represented their house at handball so that it could field a team in order not to be disqualified, despite hating ball games, PE and all of their team mates (who incidentally never passed to them once), then that is an unmitigated success – showing character and self-sacrifice for a higher cause. And just like if your pupil helps another who is upset, or learns how to do up their tie, or attends school every day for a week (when normally it would barely be a half of one), then these are nailed-on, cast-iron cases of success. All that's needed is for them to be quietly acknowledged and, with sincerity, praised. Which can be done, as the question suggests, via a once-weekly quiet conversation between pupil and form tutor. Or between pupil and you. Or with anyone, with whom your pupil is comfortable. You surely have to see that you are succeeding, sometimes against the odds, to believe that you can do more of it, in ever more varied ways.

SUMMER

What is my need in confidence and resilience?

'To share my successes with my form tutor.'

What I can do to meet this need:

'Tell sir on a tuesday about my Resilience and things I am proud of.'

My feelings about my efforts to meet my needs:

Week 1: 'I forgot to tell my form tutor but I'm confident next time.'

Week 2: 'Pleased to share my Spanish assessment result.'

Week 3: 'Came to school when I didn't want to.'

Week 4: 'told sir about my sewing cross stitch and running stitch.'

Needs met ✓

BRANDON

What is my need in confidence and resilience?

'To share my successes with my form tutor.'

What I can do to meet this need:

'Be more positive when something positive happens. Ignore people who try to wind me up. Share my successes with miss on a Wednesday.'

My feelings about my efforts to meet my needs:

Week 1: 'Told form tutor about great RE lesson and rounders lesson.'

Week 2: 'Shared food mock experience and tactic to ignore Jack who is annoying me in maths.'

Week 3: 'Feels good that someone cares and notices when I'm trying really hard every day.'

Week 4: 'Sir proud of me for completing geography homework thoroughly. I feel pretty decent about that!'

Needs partly met ✓

AM I INVOLVED IN ANY CLUBS AT SCHOOL?

A club has several key facets: it does the social thing, it does the skills thing, it does the shared enjoyment thing, it does the belonging thing. And the list of clubs at some schools is, quite simply, a remarkable thing. It can go well over two pages of A4. How do so many people find the time and willing – beyond the hours of their normal roles, not a penny of additional pay attached – to put on such extra provision for pupils?

You've regularly got clubs for all the usual sports and board games, design and technology, cooking, singing and instrument playing; you'll also have clubs for NFL, rock band, jazz band, trampolining and athletics; and if they're not varied enough, you'd not need long to find ones for maths supremos, gardeners, tent builders and budding librarians. I'm not sure how but on top of their day-to-day teaching, schools seem somehow to have morphed into PGL holidays, local community centres, Bake Off, your local church's Tuesday club, Camp America and a smatter-ing of old people's homes, all rolled into one. Were they to open their doors to the general public, there would be queues around the block on sign-up day. Long lines of enthusiasts – hip flasks and activity scrolls in hand, sleep-ing bags against science blocks – all there to get the best slots. Imagine the lease of life it would bring to some of our older citizens.

But opportunity, as we know from our former cost, can be lost on the young. So much ahead of you, in your grasp, but perhaps not the savvy, the freedom or free spirit to take advantage. Which is why this question is an important one: can pupils who sense that they might be missing something by not belonging to clubs at school – as evidenced by their circling of this need in the first place – be nudged into doing so?

As with many other questions surrounding confidence and resilience, this question can be all about the long game. Inevitably, there are good reasons why your pupil hasn't signed up for clubs thus far: social fear, lifts to and from, no friend to go with, nothing they think they're interested in, not sure where B29 is, or the 3G (or what it is), scared of the person who runs it. Even asking their tutor to provide the list that details names and times can be an ordeal. Even being able to read it is not a given. So, tread carefully because it's quite easy, on a wave of enthusiasm, to miss the key clue to the non-club-attender mystery – the one that doesn't just provide the key but does the unlocking too.

If, like one of my pupils, you go full circle over a period of weeks, many conversations had in-between, from 'I'll get the sign-up sheet from miss and check with mum' to 'I'll ask mum again' to 'I feel nervous because I don't do clubs' to 'I think I'll wait until spring' to 'I'm happy to wait until spring' to 'I think I'll just go home and play with my friends', that's OK. Your pupil has been through a process which has taught them how much they, and those around them, can be pushed right now. Yes, it would be great if they were able to join a club, a huge step in fact, but actually there were obstacles in the way, which despite the coercing, cajoling and good will on both sides, just couldn't be overcome this time around.

But the seeds have been planted. Next time, with support, they might just be able to get themselves over the line of starting with a new club. And never look back.

For the others – the lift issues, the friend issues, the social issues, the interest issues, the location issues – you know what to do: listen, explore, listen, suggest.

ETHAN

What is my need in confidence and resilience?

'Going to art club with my friend.'

What I can do to meet this need:

'Check that it is on Monday after school. Be brave and ask the teacher if I can go. Arrange getting home.'

My feelings about my efforts to meet my needs:

Week 1: 'Asked my friend to ask the art teacher.'

Week 2: 'Find out who the art teacher is. I don't like asking teachers questions but I'm going to try.'

Week 3: 'Ask grandpa if I can go.'

Week 4: 'I can't go to art club this week. I think I'll drop this. It's OK.'

Needs not met ✓

CHAPTER 5

BEHIND THE QUESTIONS: ORGANISATION AND PRESENTATION

At what point in your life do you become properly organised? And who teaches you? It's difficult not to love the gay abandon of some primary school pupils, throwing themselves at school – running in in the morning without so much as a look around at their dropper-offer; rushing out at break, mind set on only one thing – their territory of the playground, be it the climbing frame, football goals or just that familiar patch they like to occupy behind the toilets; and again at lunch, when ironically there's not actually the time or brain space to have lunch, such is their obsession with outsideness and physical expression; and then the five-to-three leg-jittering that precedes the mass lunging for coats and bags at home time – and straight back to the world of non-school and their invisible picker-upper.

Everything for them seems to happen now. There is no past or future. Life is purely present tense, and anything that deigns to be something that has happened, or might yet still, is frankly irrelevant. A footnote in history, a future history that might yet never be – like the homework due tomorrow or the spellings sheet for Friday: 'Why would I know where that is? It's not anything like Friday now. It's barely even Tuesday night, stupid!'

Such pupils represent just one personality type among many, but I wonder, actually, how prevalent this mindset is – not just across the primary years but in secondary too. However impractical, I can't help but admire it. Living for now, and screw the rest. It seems to fit with being young.

Pupils of this ilk might start shifting a little more shiftily than usual when confronted with this section – seizing the day and organisation aren't the most natural of bedfellows. However, even this happy-go-lucky pupil subset knows, in their heart of hearts, that a worksheet looked after here; a spot of revision done there; a planner unstained by blackcurrant, mud or egg sandwich; and a calculator to hand for, well, the calculator paper, makes for a happier and more productive – even if a tiny bit more boring – life.

DO I COMPLETE HOMEWORK ON TIME?

For many questions on the passport you'll need time to tease out the truth, because neither you nor your pupil will instinctively know the answer. This isn't one of them. The answer will be as plain as the question.

Homework is, let's face it, the bane of all our lives. Government tells head teacher, who tells teaching and learning director, who tells head of subject, who tells teacher, who tells pupil, who is also told by parent or carer that it must be done. So all of us do our best to ensure it is so.

The merits and demerits of homework are probably as wide-ranging as the ways in which, and the purposes for which, it is set. You can debate them, alongside children's need for a break from school and time to unwind, ad infinitum and still be no clearer on whether to keep it or lose it. But for the time being at least it's here to stay and, by the law of averages, a good chunk of it – especially when used as preparation for lessons – will be useful for pupils and parent helpers alike (who get a second education, albeit unrequested, for free).

Its perceived usefulness or otherwise, however, will have little relation to your pupil's capacity to get it done and handed in – the latter being by no means a natural product of the former. This is the organisation section, remember. And, of course, there's the small matter of willing too.

After four weeks of working on this question, with an admirably completed (if not so admirably followed) 'What

I can do to meet this need' section, Alfie, Year 7, finally came clean:

'I prefer to sit on my phone, sir.'

'Yes, I imagine you do, but ...'

'I feel like I don't care.'

And that, in a nutshell, or bombshell, becomes the final retreat of the serial non-homework-doer. It becomes such an onerous burden that each time another task is set and not done, with detentions flying around like errant fireworks, the lid closes ever more firmly on any future homework ever being done – because the doer, if they ever had any in the first place, has no will left with which to attempt any more.

Consequently, those plans to join homework club, to listen to the nags of mum and older brother, to check Show My Homework[1] once a day, to set a daily reminder alarm for 4pm, to ask when stuck, to put it in school bag when complete, they all falter at the first hurdle – which is to have enough care about doing the homework in the first place. This may be the organisation and presentation section but for now it's morphed into reflection and self-esteem.

'Why is that, do you think?'

Alfie can answer this sub-question in many different ways – from memory, it was one of those hyper-defensive I-don't-know grunts. But with time, you'll likely find that however non-homework-doing started, it is the unceasingly punitive nature of it that has chiefly ensured his continued early retirement from it. So you need to pick him up. And go again. Because in mine and Alfie's cases, in this particular example, even our building blocks were too advanced to help.

---

1   See https://www.teamsatchel.com/products/smhw.html.

If your pupil is telling you, however roundaboutly, that they need to see success and meaning in homework, and fast, then do it. You can print out one of their thousands of undone tasks and do it together; you can do two; you can liaise with the teacher and ask for a differentiated version more aligned to their skill level; you can do research; you can request a school truce – a timeout on detentions to allow time for him to catch up and feel proud (as opposed to do some, be no further ahead and still feel stigmatised); you can call home or the special educational needs (SEN) department, or both.

You can do many different things, but the one thing that is vital is that you follow up what it felt like for Alfie to get a piece of homework in, to have the teacher off his back, to have a little more idea what was happening in class, to be able to take part and receive praise, and for once not to feel like he was the outcast of the class. At a minimum, he gets a taste of the happy drug that everyone else has been living off for a while – the pride that comes from achievement, however mundane. Easier said than done, I grant you, but small steps that at least give a chance for the bigger ones being taken next.

Oh, and if for other children the completion of homework is *just* a case of being better organised, as the section name hints, then pupils tell me that a coloured folder does wonders for homework-sheet-retention, a working log-in for checking homework online, a phone alarm for homework-completion, a dirty great note on their wall for homework-making-it-into-school-bag and a tightly screwed-on drinking bottle cap for homework-preservation.

The dogs eating it, the cats pissing on it, the parents washing it, siblings igniting it, UFOs confiscating it, thin air

vanishing it, none of that can be helped – as we all remember from school, it's just a normal part of homework life.

JORDAN (CONTINUED)

What is my need in organisation and presentation?

'Complet homework on time.'

What I can do to meet this need:

'Not having help and for soneone to try and help. Ask
mom to take my phone so I do 10 min of homework.
Go to homework club go tomorrow morning at 8am.
Ask mom to wake me.'

My feelings about my efforts to meet my needs:

Week 1: 'Fell like I could do more but don't have help to
do it.'

Week 2: 'I fell very very good for rivisin with my mum.'

Week 3: 'Make bord at home to rimind me about
homework club.'

Week 4: 'I'm not completing all of my homework. Try
harder next time.'

Needs partly met ✓

Week 8 update: One month later, after first visit to
homework club, overheard excitedly explaining to
another pupil: 'I've avoided two detentions this morning. I'm so pleased I did homework club!'

KELSEY

What is my need in organisation and presentation?

'To complete homework on time.'

What I can do to meet this need:

'Start homework report to inspire me. Do it when I get it. Ask for help from dad even though he is busy.'

My feelings about my efforts to meet my needs:

Week 1: 'I haven't started but I will next week. feel OK.'

Week 2: 'Still haven't. target Mon/Wed for homework.'

Week 3: 'Brought in Proof of homework revision. me and sir are proud.'

Week 4: 'Improving. dads offered help and doing it with friends. much better report comments from teachers.'

Needs partly met ✓

Week 10 update: Several commendations and no homework detentions for the last two months.

DO I LOOK AFTER WORKSHEETS FOR SCHOOL?

No need for a conversation really. Smile sweetly and wait patiently for them to show you the inside of their bag – should they wish, of course. The zip might be broken but that could be a red herring. So too the squashed banana and dog-eared maths book. There may be some ink stains and the odd broken ruler, a couple of old sandwiches and a wet towel. But if, once more books and equipment have been tossed aside, they do make it to the bottom and there are no concertinaed sheets that have been nobly bearing all the weight, you may have your answer. Yes, they do look after their worksheets (even if little else), and what's more they're safely housed in one of the folders just ejected.

If the sheets are there at the bottom – a crumpled one from this week, a ripped one from last, a barely identifiable one from goodness knows when – there's still no need for conversation, just yet. Perhaps a little knowing shrug between you and a quiet instruction to 'Pop your things back in, thanks.'

From experience, this particular issue of organisation can be one of the quickest to solve – assuming you're well stocked with coloured folders. Again, little need for talking, just open your cupboard, fan out your range and reach for your sheet of name stickers while they pick.

The pleasure I've seen spread across faces, from 11- to 17-year-olds, as those sheets are placed in, the popper firmly popped and the name sticker stuck on, is not inconsiderable. There's a moment of 'Why didn't I think of this?' and then you both go about your business. But not before – absolutely not before – you've had the how-to-use chat. After all, no different from cars and washing machines, a folder is only useful if you know how to use it.

Here's my five-point plan:

1   Put worksheet in folder when you receive it.

2   Put folder in bag once worksheet is in it.

3   Take worksheet out to work on at home/school/on bus.

4   Once work on sheet is finished (for now), put back in folder.

5   Put folder straight back in bag.

But feel free to find your own way.

ISRAEL

What is my need in organisation and presentation?

'Look after worksheets for school.'

What I can do to meet this need:

'Get folder. Whatever the time is put sheets in it. Always have a glue stick also.'

My feelings about my efforts to meet my needs:

Week 1: 'I am gluing all my sheets in my books and putting spare sheets in folder.'

Week 2: 'Every sheet I stick in straight away. I feel good as every sheet is stuck in and easy to get to.'

Week 3: 'It's nicer to have an organised book.'

Week 4: 'It makes the book so much neater and nice looking. Nearly used an entire glue stick.'

Needs met ✓

DO I REVISE FOR
TESTS AT SCHOOL?

Probably even more importantly than the whether, for this question, is the how. As anyone who has ever tried to revise knows, revision is rarely an intuitive thing and most people have to find methods that work for them. That said, some methods are sounder than others.

But let's start with the whether. One Year 7 pupil I worked with wrote, quite matter-of-factly, on his passport: 'I've never done this in my life.' And just like some of our non-homework-doers above, I imagine he isn't alone.

Clearly, revising things you've been learning at school (or anywhere, in fact), in the pursuit of richer understanding, is a good thing. So, if your pupil chooses this question as their need, they must in some way get the fact that to start doing it, or doing more of it, or more effectively, will improve their chances of school success.

Revision should probably have a class of its own at school because, for some at least, it remains a mystery right up until the day of their final exams. But in the absence of revision lessons on the revision curriculum or embedded revision for every topic studied – and I realise that plenty of teachers do this when time permits or as part of estab-lished plans – with this question more than most, it helps to be quite prescriptive about the options available to pupils who would like to join their revising peers and retain more learning. A precis of the *Guardian*'s advice goes something like this:[2]

1　Revise school topics little and often, and always revise for tests.

2　Make, carry and use flash cards – as often as possible.

3　Ask all willing testers to test you, once you've revised.

4　Use said testers to explain your learning to – the explaining process significantly advances the learning process.

2　See B. Busch, The science of revision: nine ways pupils can revise for exams more effectively, *The Guardian* (19 April 2016). Available at: https://www.theguardian.com/teacher-network/2016/apr/19/students-revise-exams-revision-science.

5   Test yourself and deliberately create intervals between study to allow for forgetting.[3]

6   Use practice papers where applicable.

7   Quit the highlighter – it doesn't work very well.[4]

8   And the music – nor does that.[5]

9   Put your phone away. Properly. Not turned over. Nor on the side. Away. Gone. Dismissed.

10 Eat, sleep, exercise.

If you're wondering what happened to my never-revised-in-his-lifer, at some point during week 3 he recorded a personal first and revised with his mum and dad. The result? 'It was boring. It helped.'

CHEYENNE

What is my need in organisation and presentation?

'To revise for tests at school.'

What I can do to meet this need:

'Revise with sir at homework club. Ask him to test me on vocab. Make flash cards. Find websites to help me revise.'

---

3   R. Coe, C. Aloisi, S. Higgins and L. Elliot Major, *What Makes Great Teaching? Review of the Underpinning Research* (London: Sutton Trust, 2014), p. 17. Available at: https://www.suttontrust.com/wp-content/uploads/2019/12/What-makes-great-teaching-FINAL-4.11.14-1.pdf.

4   D. Cohen, Revision techniques - the good, the OK and the useless, *BBC News* (18 May 2013). Available at: https://www.bbc.co.uk/news/health-22565912.

5   N. Perham and H. Currie, Does listening to preferred music improve reading comprehension performance?, *Applied Cognitive Psychology*, 28(2) (2014). 279-284. Available at: https://onlinelibrary.wiley.com/doi/abs/10.1002/acp.2994.

My feelings about my efforts to meet my needs:

Week 1: 'Revised for Spanish test.'

Week 2: 'Revised at home for French test and again at homework club. I felt concentrated.'

Week 3: 'Revised for maths assessment. It was usefull.'

Week 4: 'I'm getting better marks. Proud of myself.'

Needs met ✓

DO I SWITCH OFF MY ELECTRONIC DEVICES AN HOUR BEFORE GOING TO SLEEP?

'Hahahahahahahahahahahaha ... HAHAHAHAHAHAHA HAHAHAHAHAHA! You're joking, sir – I sleep with it under my pillow.'

And thank goodness for the candidness of kids. We're pretty much all guilty of this one so – despite the obvious flaw in not being able to model the teaching – perhaps it's just better that we declare our hypocrisies from the start: 'OK, none of us is doing too well on this but that doesn't mean we shouldn't try. I'll turn mine off, if you do yours – just for one night before next week – and we'll compare notes then ...'

The evidence on this one is really very simple. According to the Sleep Foundation, 'Using TVs, tablets, smartphones, laptops, or other electronic devices before bed delays your body's internal clock (a.k.a., your circadian rhythm), suppresses the release of the sleep-inducing hormone melatonin, and makes it more difficult to fall asleep.' This is largely due, we learn, 'to the short-wavelength, artificial blue light that's emitted by these devices'.[6]

Electronic devices are inhibiting our children from sleeping. True, they may not be *your* children per se, but they are children over whom you have influence and whose study will suffer from a lack of said sleep. So, why not be another, or even the first, voice in their life explaining, without drama, that their device hits their sleep, which hits their focus, which hits their school life, which hits their capacity to be happy and achieve? Done. But what to do about it?

Well, there's the obvious step, heavily implied by the question – agree a good sleep time and get them to set an alarm an hour earlier to signify the halt of all electronic media, which could be coupled with some alternative suggestions such as reading or relaxation techniques. It wouldn't hurt either to 'chat with my family about our devices and ask for help with this' or 'make up some rules about when I use my phone, put them on my wall and try to stick to them'.

And if all of this is a little too cold turkey, then why not suggest, just as an interim measure, that they switch their electronic device to 'night mode', so there's minimal impact from the offending blue light.

You get the gist. We're all addicts, we all sense the consequences, we're all trying to wean ourselves off our devices, so let's do whatever we can to help.

---

6   See https://www.sleepfoundation.org/articles/why-electronics-may-stimulate-you-bed.

PRECIOUS

What is my need in organisation and presentation?

'Switch off my electronic devices an hour before going to sleep.'

What I can do to meet this need:

'Set my alarm for 9pm so I can go to bed. Read my book before I go to sleep. Dad needs too as well!'

My feelings about my efforts to meet my needs:

Week 1: 'Went to bed and read. Put alarm on.'

Week 2: 'I feel it's going well and I'm sleeping and reading well.'

Week 3: 'Mum told me to go to bed at 8.30pm and it worked.'

Week 4: 'I feel I'm sleeping well.'

Needs met ✓

DO I GET ENOUGH SLEEP AT NIGHT?

I'm sort of guessing that every teacher has had a pupil fall asleep on them in class. Mine was a Year 8 girl in English. I'm not sure whether we were reading *Skellig* or placing apostrophes – although I could take a good guess – but I knew enough about this girl to know that she likely needed the sleep. So, once it had been excitedly pointed out to me that perhaps not everyone was quite riveted by this particular session, I let her carry on: head on bag on desk. She even started lightly snoring. Once they had got over it, I distinctly remember the other pupils acclimatising to our restful friend by curbing their usual boisterousness and talking quietly around her. They got the need for sleep (and maybe they knew enough about her too).

According to Kris Gunnars at healthline.com, poor sleep is linked to heart disease, type 2 diabetes, depression and obesity.[7] Were there an educationline.com (oh, there is), advising on school-related matters such as sleep (there isn't), I'm assuming it would say that it's also linked to poor concentration, poor relationships, poor grades and solid detention numbers.

Indeed, as we all know from experience, and as any number of studies will tell us, a good day at work, school, kindergarten or Baby Bouncers is invariably, even if not exclusively, predicated on a good night's sleep. One such study, by the American Academy of Sleep Medicine, found that a lack of sleep among adolescents 'may not only contribute to lower grades and a lack of motivation, but may also increase the odds of serious levels of emotional and behavioural disturbances, including ADHD'.[8]

Interestingly, on this latter point, while other researchers agree that there can be a link between sleep deprivation and attention deficit hyperactivity disorder, they also point out that the symptoms of the two are easily confused. Psychologist Jane Ansell, who founded the charity Sleep Scotland in 1998, initially set it up to help children with special needs establish good sleeping patterns.[9]

---

7   K. Gunnars, Blue light and sleep: what's the connection?, *Healthline* (28 January 2019). Available at: https://www.healthline.com/nutrition/block-blue-light-to-sleep-better.

8   American Academy of Sleep Medicine, Poor sleep can negatively affect a student's grades, increase the odds of emotional and behavioral disturbance [press release] (9 June 2008). Available at: https://aasm.org/poor-sleep-can-negatively-affect-a-students-grades-increase-the-odds-of-emotional-and-behavioral-disturbance.

9   See https://www.sleepscotland.org.

At first, she told the BBC in 2013, people were being sent to her and 'a lot were being diagnosed as ADHD'. However, once she'd worked out a 'sleep programme' for the children which ensured they weren't sleep deprived, she found that 'some no longer had ADHD symptoms because the symptoms of hyperactivity and sleep deprivation are pretty similar'.

In order to investigate this further, Ansell coordinated pilot studies in three Scottish schools. Her findings suggested that just over half of teenagers were sleep deprived, with about a fifth reporting falling asleep in class at least once in the previous two weeks. She found that a majority of the teenagers in the study didn't realise the connection between good sleeping habits and enhanced school performance. In short: 'If you don't have enough sleep, your short-term memory doesn't consolidate into your long-term memory which is going to affect your school grades.'[10]

So, just as with the electronic-device-before-bed conundrum, my advice is to ignore the fact that you're not mum, dad, carer or guardian, and with tact, of course, always with tact, present them with the information – plus statistics, flow charts and Venn diagrams if it's more appealing; you could even make it into a mini project for them – and between you, go figure.

Other how-to-sleep-well advice for your pupil, from the aforementioned American Academy of Sleep Medicine's sleep study and a few from me, includes:

1 Set and follow a bedtime routine – same time to bed, same time to arise.

2 Avoid stimulant drinks or medicines before bed.

3 Don't go to bed hungry or after a big meal.

10 See E. Bradford, Half of teenagers sleep deprived, say experts, *BBC News* (26 August 2013). Available at: https://www.bbc.co.uk/news/uk-scotland-23811690.

4   Read or listen to audiobooks to relax.

5   Aim for nine to ten hours a night – in fact, aim for ten and you might get nine.

6   Find a sleeping position and stick to it.

7   Pop downstairs for a small bowl of (wholegrain, low-sugar) cereal when that doesn't work.

8   Request help from a professional if none of these help.

And (9), if you've not made the point clearly enough already, they might want to shut down electronic devices an hour before bed too.

MILENA (CONTINUED)

What is my need in organisation and presentation?

'To get enough sleep at night.'

What I can do to meet this need:

'Try to read before bed to replace my phone or use audiobooks to release and clear my thoughts.'

My feelings about my efforts to meet my needs:

Week 1: 'Using audiobooks is helping so far.'

Week 2: 'I think I have improved but I still have a long way to go.'

Week 3: 'I am really happy listening to audiobooks and it's helping with sleep.'

Week 4: 'I have read once but I fell asleep and I lost the page but also I done my audiobooks as well.'

Needs met ✓

DO I FOLLOW THE SCHOOL'S PRESENTATION GUIDELINES?

You'll have a good idea by now whether the answer to this question ought to be a 1, 2 or 3, almost as well as your pupil. Even writing their name on the front of the passport will be a giveaway. By the time they've filled in the date, form and transferred a few needs onto the back, the presentation question will likely be answered unequivocally.

As with spellings, I've grown to think that poor presentation is not the end of the world. If the person it is intended for and the author can read it (admittedly that's a big 'if' sometimes – more on them later), then as with the doctor's prescription and the pharmacist, that's surely all that matters?

But surely not, of course, too. The reason we often get frustrated when something doesn't look nice or becomes tainted in some way, like with a smudge or error, is because we lose self-esteem and miss out on a quick shot of pride – for living up to a standard many of us sense lurking somewhere inside. It can also mean we miss out on esteem from those around us: the regard that emanates from someone else seeing and commenting on our aesthetically appealing writing, that's another shot of pride missed too.

According to Ralph Ryback in *Psychology Today*, this isn't just a matter of appreciation, it's an issue of basic biology: 'The human body is made up of tens of thousands of integrated biological and neurochemical systems, all of which are organised. Many of our cells operate on strict schedules ... Even at the atomic level, we are well regulated and well organised.'[11]

Now, this article had nothing to do with schools. In fact, it was about as far from some pupils' lives, some heads of household might agree, as you might get: it was about keeping your home clean. However, the supposition is this: that we crave orderliness in our lives to mirror the orderliness in our bodies. Whether it's the pile of magazines overflowing on the workspace, the army of cups stopping the cupboard door from closing or the angle of the futon to the sun, its point is clear: that 'neatness and order support health – and oppose chaos'.

If by writing over the dotted line, with great angry marks streaking through errors, with capitals and lower cases strewn around randomly, and with lettering barely discernible, we are diminishing our own health, then maybe that's another good argument for trying to get our presentation a little more in order. Hence the need, irksome as it might feel – possibly to you both – to follow the school's guidelines.

It's a habit, of course, and for those of your pupils who choose this question, a habit that they will likely find very difficult to change. Hear them out, as always, discuss background and longevity, pen choice (you know, those who carry pens) and speed of writing, and see if they can't start themselves off with a few ideas about what they might do to meet this need, remembering that a piece of work neatly started tends to foreshadow one neatly continued. So, maybe they can make the neatness of the title the focus of next week's lessons (or even just the English ones)

---

11 R. Ryback, The powerful psychology behind cleanliness: how to stay organized, and reap the health benefits, *Psychology Today* (11 July 2016). Available at: https://www.psychologytoday.com/us/blog/the-truisms-wellness/201607/the-powerful-psychology-behind-cleanliness.

and ensure it's underlined with a ruler; or write the date in full rather than a scrawled number version; or slow down when the opportunity presents itself (such as now).

A short list of achievable aims to kick-start the work presentation thing can go a long way. And as with so much else, a quick return on these aims, captured at source – a tick for neatness, praise for the ruler line – will make it go even further.

For those pupils whose difficulties with presentation – your conversation or observations have revealed – would seem to be beyond issues of complacency, and there will be a good many of them, then help may be needed with their motor skills. Dyspraxia, or developmental coordination disorder (DCD) as it's sometimes called, according to understood.com, is 'a lifelong condition that makes it hard to learn motor skills and coordination'.[12] Such as writing. There are conflicting opinions on its origins but, as the Dyspraxia Foundation explains, 'it is thought to be caused by a disruption in the way messages from the brain are transmitted to the body', which 'affects a person's ability to perform movements in a smooth, coordinated way'.[13]

Regardless, it is a well-recognised condition and one that can be explored by relevant healthcare professionals. To get to them, your first port of call is your SEN team or your pupil's form tutor or their parent/carer. Or maybe their head of year. In fact, only you know your best port of call because, as is often the case, it's not necessarily the position or role of the person that counts; it's their capacity and willingness to do that aspect of their job in a way that can benefit the child. A quick chat with the right person could be invaluable for your pupils.

---

12 See https://www.understood.org/en/learning-thinking-differences/child-learning-disabilities/dyspraxia/understanding-dyspraxia.

13 See www.dyspraxiafoundation.org.uk.

While we're thinking about recognised learning disorders, it's worth noting also, as the Dyspraxia Foundation tells us on its website, that although dyspraxia does occur in isolation, it regularly presents alongside other conditions too, such as Asperger's syndrome, ADHD, dyslexia, dysgraphia and language disorders. So, that conversation with the SEN team could be even more important at this point.

If only your school knew what its presentation guidelines were getting themselves into.

HOW WELL DO I LOOK AFTER MY PLANNER?

The physical manifestation of organised life, planners, had to go in this section. Up until recently, they have been very useful for pupils to write their homework in, to carry notes between parent and teacher (such as why homework is not done), to work out which day of the week it is and whether the week is even or odd, on what day half-term will arrive and various other little conveniences. Not only that, but it has also been the trusted storage home for all manner of school rules ranging from uniform-wearing and hairstyles to bullying and detention acquisition.

However, it feels like planners and the like are fast becoming obsolete. Show My Homework et al. have thankfully taken over the homework storage mantle – a great invention for pupils and an even greater one for parents. Messages can now be sent via email, term-time info and holiday dates are plastered all over school websites, and commendations and detentions are now recorded virtually – a simple system for which various noble sticker schemes have had to give way.

Your pupil might be inclined to ask in reply to this question, 'Why should I even look after my planner?' Or, for the less confrontational, a quiet shrug that says, 'I've lost it' or 'No one asks for it any more,' or maybe even, 'I've tried to buy one three times but the school hasn't got any left.'

It's not looking like too clever a question, is it? But it is chosen sometimes, and that is of course because, while the planner still exists, it is symbolic of the wider organisation and presentation issue: can your pupil look after an item of schoolware? Is it something they can remember to bring into school and not leave on the side? Are they able to use it to make notes about schoolwork or responsibilities? To record dates of music lessons, interventions and outside appointments? Can they own it without desecrating it from front cover to back? Could they produce it right now, if asked?

If no, no, definitely no, don't know, er ... no and er ... no again, then you're on to a winner. Set small targets together, check in each week and watch as the planner slowly helps your pupil to find their organisational and presentational way. Virtual commendations for achievement go without saying.

DO I TAKE TIME TO EAT A GOOD BREAKFAST?

This is a strangely popular question, I've found. It reveals all sorts of interesting titbits from home – and, yes, before you ask, it does often feel intrusive. And, yes again, parents quite rightly bristle when you talk about it with them and their child at parents' evening or on similarly opportune occasions. In my experience, parents and carers regularly do everything in their power to enable their child to have something decent to eat in the mornings. And in my experience also, once discussed, they quickly realise that you aren't accusing them of anything – merely asking for support with what their child perceives as a need that is not being met, and nine times out of ten through no fault of the parents or carers.

As mentioned in Chapter 3, it is one of several – or many, depending on your viewpoint – passport questions which blur the line between school and home. And it's not for me to convince you that this is a conversation you should feel comfortable with. Indeed, if it isn't – and this goes for any of the questions suggested – please leave it out of your passport; your comfort with questions is paramount.

For me personally, it can be a key area of discussion because, with the possible exception of sleep, it feels like the vital component of a good school day. As a study by researchers at the University of Leeds suggests, it has few peers when it comes to importance for school performance. Surveying 294 students from schools and colleges in West Yorkshire, it found that those who never ate breakfast or ate it only occasionally (just under half) performed considerably less well academically than their breakfast-eating peers. Indeed, for those who skipped it altogether, their grades were almost two grades lower (after accounting for factors such as socio-economic status, ethnicity, age, sex and body mass index).[14]

As inferred above, for whatever reason, plenty of students like talking about this question. 'Oh no, I don't have time for breakfast – I barely have time to put my uniform on,' 'Yeah, I grab a coffee and a biscuit on my way out some-times' and, my personal favourite from a week 1 reflection,

---

14 K. Adolphus, C. L. Lawton and L. Dye, Associations between habitual school-day breakfast consumption frequency and academic performance in British adolescents, *Frontiers in Public Health*, 7 (2019): 283. Available at: https://www.frontiersin.org/articles/10.3389/fpubh.2019.00283/full.

'I didn't take time to eat a good breakfast this week but I will after Christmas.'

As they do like talking about it, it's a great opportunity to share good scientific facts. As with the sleep topic, you can be another person in their life to let them know that the nutritional value of a biscuit (unlike its calorific one) is negligible; that coffee stimulates by tricking the body's nervous system, that children are more sensitive to its effects and that stimulants are addictive; that a croissant, muffin or scone with butter is OK as a treat but not as a staple breakfast; that cereal might fill a hole but it often contains a lot of sugar (even more, the higher up it appears on the ingredients list) which when consumed in too high a daily quantity can lead to being overweight and at an increased risk of diabetes; and, anyway, have they tried porridge or a quality muesli or fresh fruit or wholemeal toast for breakfast?

And, yes, I know that for every report which claims that eggs are great, another will claim otherwise, so you'll be in knots explaining that protein is good for bones and muscles, but too many might raise cholesterol, and the white is great for this, but the yolk might be bad for that, and where do eggs come from anyway, and – you're kidding me – the unfertilised product of a hen's ovaries, and where should I buy them, and who bred the chicken, and in what conditions, and under whose auspices? But if you stick to the clearer-cut basics – you know, like slower-release fruit sugars being better for you (and your energy levels) than faster-release biscuit ones – then you can only enrich their understanding and put them in better stead to make a better choice the next time they find their way to that all too elusive breakfast table.

Clearly, this section could open a can of worms. Choosing what, when and if to eat, as we all know, isn't just about whether your tummy is rumbling. If so, I'd say that's a good thing. Maybe a red flag will appear over your student's eating habits; one they quietly want you to find out about – an opportunity to get on top of something that wouldn't have been available through conventional means. Remember also that it's their self-chosen need – an area they would like to address with help from you. It's a compliment as well as an opportunity. Hear them out, take them seriously, be humble and don't catastrophise. Our expertise may not lay in eating psychology but it does lay in listening and suggesting. Ideally, you can agree the next steps together but, of course, if you feel a child is at risk because of what they've told you, as in all matters of child welfare, you know the channels to pursue.

However, in most cases this will be about the utterly mundane – alarm not set early enough, got bored of Shreddies, no chocolate spread left, porridge too time-consuming, no idea how to make it anyway, got out of the breakfast habit, no time to feed me *and* the cat, need to be out of the house too early, canteen's doughnuts quicker and tastier – so maybe check out (below) a few of the ideas students have come up with on how to inspire habit change.

CHARLIE

What is my need in organisation and presentation?

'Take time to eat a good breakfast and try new foods.'

What I can do to meet this need:

'I don't really eat breakfast. I'm going to try pineapple this week, apple next, mango week after and raspberrys. Target [set by pupil himself]: cut a piece of apple and try it.'

My feelings about my efforts to meet my needs:

Week 1: 'I'm disappointed I need try to attempt this need.'

Week 2: 'Tried apple and didn't like it. I will try pineapple next. Still disappointed. Target: remind mum to bye pineapple.'

Week 3: 'I tried a pineapple and didn't like it. I will try mango next.'

Week 4: 'I'm eating waffles and syrup for breakfast but will try to add fruit as well.'

Needs partly met ✓

KAI

What is my need in organisation and presentation?

'Take time to have breakfast.'

What I can do to meet this need:

'Set [weekday] alarm for 7.15am instead of 7.45am. Be quicker in the morning so I have time to eat breakfast.'

My feelings about my efforts to meet my needs:

Week 1: 'I feel pleased because I had breakfast.'

Week 2: 'Ate breakfast and proud with myself.'

Week 3: 'I feel I do more work when I had breakfast.'

Week 4: 'I am eating breakfast for four weeks. It is good.'

Needs met ✓

DO I DRESS NEATLY AND APPROPRIATELY FOR SCHOOL?

A little bit like the planner question, this one feels like it may become more archaic the more our society changes. But, for now, whether you have a school uniform, no uniform or what feels like a half-uniform, the heart of the question is whether your pupil is abiding by what has been asked.

For this reason, it would appear to be a good opportunity for a debate about uniform and presentation: about how it impacts on freedom of expression; whether it does or doesn't impact on learning, and if so, how; about pupils' school obligations. As this could be a long and interesting debate, should you have the time, it might also be a good opportunity to talk about (a) the benefits and disadvantages of conformity and its future relevance to pupils' adult lives, and (b) the importance – where important to those involved – of lawful challenge and protest.

It might lead to nothing, to a letter, to a meeting or even to a quiet demonstration, as it did for some boys at Isca Academy in Exeter during the summer of 2017.[15] With the help of their female peers, 30-odd teenage boys turned up at school in grey box-pleat skirts in protest at the rule which insisted they wear full-length trousers all year round. Credit to the pupils, no matter their gender, and also to the school, which responded to what it presumably judged as a reasonable request delivered in an appropriate way, with the prompt introduction of a new rule that they could wear tailored charcoal grey shorts during the next academic year's summer term. A fitting case of an

---

15 R. Adams, Exeter school's uniform resolve melts after boys' skirt protest, *The Guardian* (23 June 2017). Available at: https://www.theguardian.com/education/2017/jun/23/exeter-schools-uniform-resolve-melts-after-boys-skirt-protest.

important topic having the airtime to breathe and be heard, and a fine victory for emotional intelligence all round.

And, no, you're not trying to incite a riot. And yes, your head teacher (unlike Isca's) may end up very fed up with you. But if this passport is worth anything, and even if this would appear to be just a question about clothing, it is surely worth the even-handed discussion and investigation into issues that are based on values that affect decision-making that affect change. Just because your school sets a value that pupils should dress neatly and appropriately, doesn't mean it can't be discussed or even challenged – neat and appropriate are subjective terms, after all. The time might just be ripe for it to be re-examined. In any case, what is learning if it's not, in some way, about pushing boundaries?

On that note, for the large majority of cases, you can drop the *Dead Poets Society* daydream and put together a few words about how – notwithstanding a grand future pro-test involving all local schools and media outlets – for the time being at least, your pupil might want to pull their tie a bit tighter, wear their skirt a bit longer, their shirt a bit more in (and less out) of their trousers, don their blazer a little more often, quit with the red socks thing, decorate their hands a little less liberally, and stop somehow misunderstanding the difference between a trainer and a shoe. That will help to get the highlighter pen more liberally spread across the section.

AM I ON TIME FOR LESSONS?

Plenty of students have spells, or occasions, of being late – the deliberate ones, not the accidental variety. But this question is more about the serial offenders. The ones whose school identity almost depends on a later class-room arrival than the rest, which will either remain as just that or kick on to include a minor disruption, or indeed a full-blown one affecting teacher, student and the general class ambience. As all teachers know how difficult it can be to settle a class after transition, they know the importance of this question.

For their part, the student will have less of an appreciation, so as part of your discussion, why not furnish them with one, along the lines of 'Let's walk in your teacher's shoes ...' And once you've educated them about the time it takes to prepare lessons, to plan starters and plenaries and the middle stuff, to mark books and set targets and differenti-ate, and the skill required to settle a group of 29, after PE or break, and the effect of lateness on others' learning, then you'll have provided them with the opportunity to wonder and reflect, and maybe even empathise.

I say maybe because empathy is a learned art. The more you are encouraged, the more likely you are to do it. And the less, the less likely. Yes, it perhaps ought to be a sensed thing, a skill born of intuition, selflessness and true care – not one spelled out for you because you're too caught up in your own world to notice – but I'm guessing few have that to start with, and we've all got to start somewhere. So, whatever your (joint) ideas might involve in terms of what your student can do to meet this need, should your words have resounded, these ideas will include a sentence reflecting a dose more thought for their class and teacher.

For the student with poor timekeeping – no malice, just poor timekeeping – this ought to be an easier conundrum for you both to solve. Although don't be surprised if telling the time on the school's analogue clocks turns out to be their issue; they won't be the first Year 7 or 11 to struggle.

But they may be one of the first, at secondary school at least, to learn how.

HOW OFTEN DO I ATTEND SCHOOL?

It won't be news to you that, by and large, those who attend most do best; and those who don't, well, don't. It may be news to your student, however – so don't be afraid to share with them findings such as those from the Department for Education, which in February 2015 published findings that two years of blemishless GCSE class attendance resulted in 44% of pupils achieving the English Baccalaureate. This figure fell to 31.7% for those who had up to two weeks of absence during the same period, and to 16.4% for those who had up to double that fortnight.[16]

Share them not so much as to frighten them, as to educate them in the importance of being educated. Every day. Without reasonable exception. And that exceptions can become habits. And that if their exceptions become habits, at the same time as other variables – such as the education system not always managing to put a trained subject teacher in front of them – then opportunities for happiness, self-esteem and future personal success may diminish likewise.

But before doing so, of course, listen to what they have to say – their routines (or lack thereof), their habits, their journeys, their happiness levels, their motivation and, most importantly, their view of education and all it has come to mean to them. Voiced and listened to, you'll both feel wiser – about the nature and extent of the issues, and about the

---

16 S. Weale, Missing lessons harms children's education, says UK government, *The Guardian* (22 February 2015). Available at: https://www.theguardian.com/education/2015/feb/22/missing-lessons-harms-childrens-education-uk-government.

actions your student may be able to take to help improve attendance. As an educator, you'll know that eight-and-a-half times out of ten, a self-esteem-based reward for improvement – however small – will be well received and serve as a tender incentive for future improvements. So, if you've got an eight-and-a-half-er, make good use of them.

Of course, there could be extenuating circumstances at play, such as issues at home – your conversation with them, or indeed a prior or consequent one with their form tutor, should alert you to such. In which case, maybe you can help. Could a kind ear with home soften a stance? Could the school do more to assist? Should a fellow professional be alerted? Use all the clues to make easier the how-to question.

But it may be that unauthorised absence has just become the norm for this particular student – despite overall absence rates seeing a marked improvement since halfway through the first decade of this century, for the year 2017–2018 the unauthorised absence rate in all schools was as its highest since records began (in 2006–2007)[17] – so a clever strategy will be needed. There is no silver bullet, but the sum of all your joint strategies – it is, after all, a need your school-shy friend has chosen to work on – may just pick up this student's attendance rate.

---

17 Department for Education, Pupil absence in schools in England: 2017 to 2018 (21 March 2019). Available at: https://assets.publishing.service.gov.uk/government/uploads/system/uploads/attachment_data/file/787463/Absence_3term_201718_Text.pdf.

AM I PREPARED FOR EACH LESSON WITH THE RIGHT EQUIPMENT AND BOOKS?

Am I hell. This will be as plain as day to both of you. Because your student either flashed their trusty biro when you asked them, or they didn't; and they either located their special highlighter pen in their pencil case, or they didn't; and they either found it easy to produce their report card or planner or homework folder, or they didn't.

You can be forgiven for cutting to the chase on this one. Perhaps with humour. Or with empathy. Or with both. Either will help, I'm sure, in evoking a confessional purge which will make your student feel a lot better in themselves, even if not in their organisation.

Being more organised will likely involve taking responsibility, having methods (not adults) to draw on and about having practice with those methods. Occupational therapist and educator Victoria Prooday cites six organisational strategies to help 'turn on' a child's brain:

- Teach them to use a calendar.
- Make a checklist for daily routines.
- Use a reward points system for good stuff (as opposed to negative comments for bad).
- Help with organisational aids such as folders.
- Involve the student in instruction-following activities.
- Let your child fail and face the consequences of their disorganisation.[18]

---

18 V. Prooday, When children are disorganized: reasons & solutions (2 November 2017). Available at: https://yourot.com/parenting-club/2017/11/22/when-children-are-disorganized-reasons-solutions.

Anyone who has got children will know that this last one in particular is hard. But as it's not your child, you may just find it easier to leave the PE kit they've left behind in your room at the end of the session where it is, and not hare down the corridor after them to save them getting a detention and having to play handball in the school's manky spare kit.

Just previous to this brilliant learning opportunity, though, discuss and write down a few practicable steps in the how-to section. But at the same time, if the case seems severe, as with presenting work neatly, don't rule out a possible dyspraxia – because, according to the Dyspraxia Foundation, students with this type of motor impairment will be 'unable to remember and/or follow instructions' and will be 'generally poorly organised'.[19] In short, looking after and finding stuff is the tallest of orders in itself.

But not impossible. As one such young man reflected on week 2 concerning his feelings about his efforts to meet his needs: 'My teacher says I've improved. I haven't noticed … I only lost one pair of shoes in the last week though. It's a start.'

---

10 See www.dyspraxiafoundation.org.uk

CHAPTER 6

BEHIND THE QUESTIONS: ATTITUDE TO LEARNING

Or AtL, as teachers like to call it. These three letters have taken off so well in some schools that there are even leagues for them: pupils ordered by attitude. The season starts off, presumably, like all sporting seasons, with participants well rested and energised, and even if they've carried out little pre-season training, you can be sure they will be full of good intentions to perform right at the top of their games from the off. The opening weeks ensue and the jostling begins. A few quickly assume their mantle at the top of the table, as do a few at the foot, so for the rest it's about competing for the other spots. By about week 10, just like in recent Premier League seasons, a clearer picture emerges: neither Blossom Knight nor Liverpool are ever likely to relinquish top spot or second; Jacob King and Norwich, or Huddersfield, will be lucky to get out of the bottom two; the bottom half will largely stay in the bottom half; the top half in the top.

We all revert to type, right? And if that's right, then maybe, regardless of the hopes and dreams and aspirations of any one individual or team, it's the psychology of feeling capable of achieving a finite amount of things, with a finite amount of ability, and a finite amount of effort, in a finite amount of time that is most at play when we perform as we are, well, predestined to do. Because of our background, our parents, our cleverness (as a rigid perception), our class; because of our players, our manager, our owner, the amount we spent on new signings

But then there's Leicester 2016.[1] And Wimbledon 1988.[2] There's even Melchester Rovers.[3] OK the last one's not real but it is to my 9-year-old self. Predestination, it would appear, in fiction as well as non-fiction, only self-fulfils when the predestinee accepts their own predestination. The attitude to learning section, not unlike the first two sections, is one small opportunity to resist that.

Pupils who rarely pay attention can learn how; those who call out can refrain from so doing; those who self-castigate for even the smallest of errors can learn to give themselves a break. 5,000-1 shot Leicester can win the league. Lowly Wimbledon can beat Liverpool in the FA Cup Final. Melchester Rovers can come from three nil down to win 4-3 in the last minute – with half the team on crutches. The odds may have been set heavily against them; they just needed self-belief, encouragement, opportunity and to

---

1 Leicester City won the Premier League in the 2015–2016 season. Their squad cost just under £55 million – by far the lowest of all top four teams. Manchester City, who came fourth, spent just under £420 million on theirs. Leicester were 5,000-1 outsiders to win the league at the start of the season, having somehow avoided relegation the previous year – they had been bottom of the table, seven points adrift of their closest rivals, with less than two months of the season left to play.

2 Wimbledon beat Liverpool 1-0 in the 1988 FA Cup Final – one of the biggest shocks in the history of the competition. Wimbledon had just finished their second season in the Football League First Division, and had been playing in the Southern Football League, the seventh and eighth tier of English football, 11 years earlier. Liverpool were the giants of English football in the 1980s and were on course to become the first team to win the Double twice, after already winning their seventeenth league title a little earlier that season.

3 Melchester Rovers were the club featured in football comic strip *Roy of the Rovers*, which ran from 1954 to 1993. It followed the ups and downs of the team and its captain, Roy Race, from season to season. The comic yielded the stock media phrase, 'Roy of the Rovers stuff', which describes sporting results or moments which go very much against the odds.

work out how. The luck bit, I suspect, was born of the other four. This is your pupil's opportunity, with your encouragement, to work out how.

DO I PAY ATTENTION IN CLASS?

I lied earlier. Unlike other sections, this one begins (in my head at least) at five past one. It kicks off a right-sided arc of questions which rather pointedly query whether your pupil is altogether very well behaved and focused. More than other questions, I feel, for those with a somewhat poor track record, these ones come loaded with pre-judgement. Of course, that's not how they're intended, but perhaps be prepared for some extra bristling and a dose of self-denial.

There are a lot of variables involved in this question, most of which involve your pupil, their classroom, their classmates and their teacher. There's your pupil's capacity to pay attention; there's their classmates' capacities to do likewise; albeit to a lesser extent, there's the geography – the attention-friendliness – of the classroom; and, of course, there's the capacity of the teacher to hold the attention of said pupils in said classroom. In summary, there's a lot that can go wrong.

I was advised by an incumbent, when I was first deciding whether to move into teaching, that there were two things that you couldn't be if you wanted to become a teacher. One was boring – no, I mean, literally, that you couldn't be boring – and the other I can't remember. I wish I could because I've since come to realise how good a piece of advice this was: my worst lessons have invariably been my most boring, for which I accept full blame. Your teacher can fail to hold your attention, of that we're all agreed.

We can also agree, I'm sure, that the other pupils around you can take your attention away. General noise levels (high or otherwise), random body noises (inadvertent or otherwise), eye and body contact, smells, jokes, conversation, tapping, ticking, tutting, clucking are all distractions which will tend to emanate from your fellow would-be learners.

The problem, of course, with both of these attention-sappers (the teachers and the other pupils) is that they might also be masks for your own inability to concentrate. That your teacher is or was boring may or may not be true; that your classmates are or aren't distracting likewise; but without your own concentration being fully up to scratch, it's impossible to know who's the chicken and who's the egg. You might have such shocking concentration that a smear on the window of the classroom is enough to distract.

Therefore, with so many variables at stake, a good place to start is with your pupil looking in their own backyard before they have even started to inspect other people's. Nudge them to reflect to that effect: 'Without anything much to distract you, are you able to concentrate? In space and quiet and with something you have to attend to – even if it's boring – can you actually attend to it? Like some elements of your homework? Or an exam you have to do? Or a form you need to fill out?'

If the answers to these questions are begrudging yeses, I'd argue that we can move to plan A: 'You can concentrate when you need to, even if something doesn't interest you. You have no deficit. You are just more attentive to things you like doing – quite normal. Your challenge is to develop interests in things you don't think you're interested in. And, yes, that does mean in your lessons. And, yes, that does include physics [sorry, physics teachers]. And geography [likewise]. Or whatever your chosen lesson of eye-straining boredom. So, how are we going to do that?'

Obviously, you're not expecting too much of an answer here. Not just yet, anyway. But if we've agreed thus far that beauty and success are in the eyes of their beholders, then I think we can probably add interest to that too. So, get your pupil to choose a lesson they are particularly inattentive in and prompt them to self-reflect.

'What do you find boring about it? What might help you to get into it? Have you normally eaten before attending it? What modes of learning do you enjoy most? In what conditions do you work best? Can you do more homework for that subject? Or do it better? Do you need help with it? Can you ask me for help? Or your teacher? Or for me to enlist other help? Have you ever been successful in that subject? At any time, including outside school? What did it look like? And feel like? Would you quite like that feeling again? Are you, generously speaking, not altogether put-ting your best into this subject? Fair enough. Why don't we try to change that and see what it yields?'

'Hmm, OK then', or maybe even a shrug, might not sound or look too encouraging, but even *that* is a place to start more advanced than the one you were in at the start of your conversation.

However, if through chats with the special needs coordi-nator or class or form teacher, if through this chat with this pupil this minute, if through all of these ifs together it would appear that your pupil's lack of attention is an issue beyond effort, then it's time for plan B, which may involve a condition you'll be familiar with: ADHD.

Attention deficit hyperactivity disorder divides teachers and parents, and indeed children, like few other four-letter abbreviations. It seems upheld and vilified in equal meas-ure. It also divides clinicians, so we're perhaps in some limbo here. But it would appear to me that the majority expert view is not dissimilar to that of Thomas E. Brown, clinical psychologist and associate professor of psychiatry at the Keck School of Medicine of the University of Southern California, who contributes to www.understood. org, a website set up in 2014 to share understanding in learning and thinking differences. A precis of some of his thoughts are as follows:

- ADHD is a brain condition and not a behavioural one.

- The make-up of the brain is significantly different in those who have it.

- It can affect absolutely anyone, irrespective of intelligence.

- People who have it fall in and out of focus.

- They do that even more when there are distractions around them.

- They often have no problem paying attention to a few things that really interest them – or to avoid something very unpleasant happening ...

- ... even though they find it incredibly difficult to pay attention to almost everything else.

- They don't have less willpower. See the first bullet point – their brain is wired differently.

- They often struggle to organise themselves ...

- ... as well as their writing. They have the ideas but can't easily organise them into sentences.

- They struggle to regulate emotion – issues take on a life of their own.

- Their long-term memory is way better than their short; it's there but they can't always retrieve it.

- They struggle to control their actions – they don't always think ahead, so tend to blunder in.

- There's a high chance it's inherited from somewhere in the family.[4]

If you're now thinking that some items on that list describe pretty much every one of us at some time or other, then snap. The question is to what degree is each of the above true and to what extent do they affect your pupil's every-day life. If in both cases the answer is pretty emphatic, then you at least have a working theory, even if you're

---

4   T. E. Brown, ADHD Explained: A 28-Minute Primer [video], *Understood.org* (2016). Available at: https://www.understood.org/en/learning-thinking-differences/child-learning-disabilities/add-adhd/adhd-explained-a-28-minute-primer?_ul=1*6w1pkr*domain_userid*YW1wLVNsdERGczl6SGlu ZlFJS0tVU2VZXQE.

unsure how to proceed. In which case, the next step is to pass on your thoughts to someone who would know, or who knows someone who would know, or who knows enough to know how to broach the issue with someone who doesn't know but, in your (plural) judgement, really ought.

It would appear that with a working, accurate diagnosis of ADHD, a young person's life can change beyond all recognition. Firstly, it can provide a level of understanding for them, their families and school staff which, even at a basic level, can obviously be a huge relief to the child and others involved. Secondly, it can pave the way for properly adjusted medication which it seems, in many cases, can significantly improve the faults in the brain processes which cause the aforementioned deficits. Thirdly, and perhaps most crucially, it can help to inspire a knowledgeable support network around the child to do the things that medication can't – helping them to develop skills and coping strategies; to recognise and strengthen their existing strengths (of which they are often painfully unaware); to combat and improve their weaknesses (of which they are often painfully aware); to reduce the reactions of parents and teachers that inadvertently exacerbate the condition, and instead make way for ones that help it.

Should you or I have judgements on the morality of medication, on the upbringing, personality or behaviour of the child, they are largely irrelevant here. Even though the condition was only given its current name as recently as 1980, it has presumably been around forever. Adam or Eve may well have had it – in fact, that would explain a lot. The Romans undoubtedly had it. And if Zeus or some of his divine peers didn't have it, then I'm a Greek god. Mr Evanes.

We live in ever more understanding times, backed up by reams and reams of science-based research – scientists, like our friend Dr Brown, somehow know things like how many neurons we have in our brains (100 billion, give or take). It behoves me, it behoves you, to help the under-standers to practise their understanding to the betterment of our children, unobstructed by our presumed wisdom.

ORHAN

What is my need in attitude to learning?

'Pay more attention in class.'

What I can do to meet this need:

'Look at the work on the board, don't look behind me. Listen and put my hand up more. Ignore anyone dis-tracting me.'

My feelings about my efforts to meet my needs:

Week 1: 'I did this when I was reminded in English. Need to practise in science.'

Week 2: 'I am doing this a lot in English and not get-ting distracted.'

Week 3: 'I've been looking at my work and not being distracted.'

Week 4: 'My English teacher said she is very happy with my work. Still need to practise in science.'

Needs partly met ✓

HOW WELL DO I REFLECT ON MY TEACHERS' COMMENTS?

'Come again?'

'Well, I suppose what this question is asking is how much do you think about the things your teacher either asks, suggests or tells you to do, such as when they mark your work or when they address you?'

'Oh.'

Reflecting on comments is a very imprecise science. How long is a reflect? Five seconds? Ten? A full chin-stroking minute? What does it constitute? Uninterrupted thoughts about only that thing, that comment? Plus resolution to act or change? Plus resolution to think about acting or changing? Plus no resolution but a little bit of reluctant acknowledgement of said comment? Or just uninter-rupted thoughts plus decision to ignore the teacher because they've no idea how to help you anyway, they keep calling you Jake when your name's clearly Jack, they've only spoken to you once all year and you'll be the arbiter of whether your writing needs more detail added to it, thank you very much.

I guess the wider point is how much your pupil is thinking about their learning – as seen through the eyes of their teacher – and to what extent have they become immune to most or all feedback. Have they become immune, for example, because to their mind it's just the same old scrawly red ink on a tethered yellow marking sticker? Or is it because it's the same verbal rebukes and warnings they've heard a hundred times before – and will a hundred more – with neither them nor the teacher having time or energy enough to break the cycle?

If they are able to recall, with some ease, examples of feedback they've received and taken on board recently, then I think that is evidence enough to highlight a 2 or a 3 and move on. It will likely be indicative of a wider habit. If, on the other hand, erms, wells, likes and sorts of pepper their reply, with discernible examples few and far between, it would obviously appear that this is an area of pupil need – and therefore an ideal place to economise on the highlighter ink.

HOW WELL DO I ACT ON THOSE REFLECTIONS TO IMPROVE MY WORK?

If the previous question didn't need a little explaining, I'm pretty confident this one will – these are slightly tricky concepts. Reflecting, as mentioned, is not something you can easily put your finger on. Acting on something is at least picturable, but how many different ways of acting on something can you think of? If you stack all those mental images on top of your wispy reflection ones, you've got yourself a bit of a mental mash-up.

It is advisable, therefore, to give examples:

- If a teacher suggests ways of writing with improved punctuation, do you spend time (a) thinking about it, (b) doing it or (c) doing it consistently?

- If a member of staff suggests personalised ways of revising for tests, do you, similarly, spend time doing (a), (b) or (c)?

- If a teacher instructs you repeatedly to use a ruler to underline titles and a pen to write them in, with a fully written date to the side, do you pay lip service to (a), rarely think about (b) or go nowhere near (c) with a barge pole?

Your pupil's answers to any one of these, or similar examples, should tell you both what you need to know. If it's a straight 0 or a wobbly 1 on the highlighter front, then this is a need well worth attending to – committing to action to self-improve is something none of us finds easy.

So, make a plan in the usual passport way. The more reflectively inactive the child, the more simple the first reflection act should be to achieve. And in the kindest, most supportive way possible, don't let the scoundrels off the hook until they've realised that on the first self-improvement issue you both choose, like for the old man in Hemingway's *The Old Man and the Sea*, it's going to take something extremely special to make you let go.

HOW WELL DO I ACT ON INSTRUCTIONS IN CLASS?

This one obviously follows closely in the footsteps of the former:

- If you're told to stop talking, do you do it – even if it's a whole-class instruction and not everyone complies?

- If you're told not to call out, do you (plus the same caveat above) do it?

- If you're instructed to hand out the books, wipe the board, take a message or sit down ... or to stop looking out the window, playing with Anil's pen, swinging on your chair or holding your head in your hands ... or to stop bashing it repeatedly on the table, lying on the floor, yawning noisily or shouting out 'I'm so bored, bored, bored,' ... do you do it?

● And how well do you manage to curtail your inactions on your teachers' instructions thereafter?

We've discussed previously how to try to separate, for the purposes of possible solutions, the child who is in bad habits from the child who has preconditions affecting their capacity to comply with, in this case, instruction-following. Work out which pupil you have on your hands and act accordingly. Whether you end up talking to other interested parties and proceeding from there, or you both end up putting together some ideas on how your pupil can meet their own needs to act on others' instructions, you will at least have started to tackle this one key aspect of your pupil's attitude to their learning.

HOW WELL DO I BEHAVE IN CLASS?

Pupils tend to get this question instinctively, even though it seems a little unfair in its lack of specificity.

What on earth is behaving in class? Yes, it's pretty much listening and working, but beyond that what does it look like? And the problem with this question, of course, is that it can look like completely different things, depending on which member of staff your pupil is with.

While one teacher will allow you to work while chatting or listening to music, another will insist on silence; while one will accept language without pleases or thank-yous, another will insist on them; while one will tolerate walking around the classroom and shouting out, another will work with neither; while one will accept backchatting, another won't; while one will have a volume of voice for every classroom situation, another will respond agreeably to pretty much any level; and while one will encourage you to form a human pyramid while singing the numbers one to twenty in French to the tune of 'Frère Jacques', not a risk assessment in sight, another will make you learn German grammar in silence. *Keine Frage*.

For children – at least, those for whom fairness and consistency is paramount – this endless source of aberration, however minor, doesn't always work. And yet it does. Because instinctively they know that we're all different. They also know that despite school rules on everything – including acceptable lengths at which to wear their skirt, tie and earrings – teachers, like parents, have different ways of doing things. And that regardless of the difference of each member of staff's approach, and regardless of the suitability of that approach to their style of learning or way of behaving, that the sometimes unwritten rule of school rules is to 'act as the situation demands, in the best interests not just of you but of those around you'.

Now, in the same way that teachers will be teachers, and by consequence they will be different, pupils will be pupils, and by consequence they will be subversive. And difficult. And non-compliant. Especially when they see an opportunity they can exploit or an inconsistency they feel hard done by. To understand this dichotomy is half the battle, maybe more. But the good news, as mentioned above, is that the vast majority of children get this already. They are highly attuned, intuitive creatures.

It's just that they don't always want to have to admit it. Because to admit to this dichotomy, to openly recognise that no two people can act in the same way towards them, however hard they try, is to accept that they too have responsibility. And to admit that is to accept that they too have work to do to make it work. And, worst of all, to admit that is to accept a fundamental point of life: that there's unfairness in the world, some of which will be necessarily unfair to them. And we're asking this of our young people who rightly believe – however little they practise it some-times – that the world just should be fair.

Which is why it's such a power play, this fight between what is and what should be, in an ideal world. So, get your pupil to see what they instinctively know already: that behaving is as much about adapting to different adults as it is about any one single act of behaviour. Walk them through that inner truth and help them to realise the unfairness of their own handling of these situations, sometimes.

They will know if they should highlight 1, 2, 3 or none of the above. However, they will also likely give you a hoard of reasons why it's not always their fault. You are allowed to empathise with this, of course – we all know that different tolerance levels can cause confusion. But the trick is to try to help them see that regardless of whose perceived fault it is, they can develop skills which will help them to adapt and to learn in class. Not just about angles or the Tudors or quantum physics, but about how to get on in life through understanding and self-management (how certain Tudors could have done with that themselves). And that learning can start right here, right now.

That said, if you think or know that there is a learning or personality difficulty, one recognised by name or behav-ioural research (and in plenty of cases there will be), then once again you need a plan B – which starts with whom-soever you judge best suited to take it forward with understanding and care.

DO I AVOID CALLING OUT IN CLASS?

I'm going to refer you to the relevant parts of the questions above here – you'll know what they are. But I'll also add this: if we're agreed as a general principle of life, let alone teaching, that all behaviour is a form of communication, then calling out is no different from any other such act. Your joint quest, of course, is to find out what it is your student is so doggedly but unproductively trying to communicate.

The first step is to identify the catalyst. Do they know many of the answers but don't get chosen? Do they know none of the answers but still want to be noticed? Do they know only a handful of the answers and are never chosen when they would desperately love to be? Could they not give two figs about the answers and enjoy expressing this at will? Are answers irrelevant to them because calling out is what you do in class, regardless of whether there's been a question or not? Especially if it's French, period 5, with a supply, who doesn't speak French. Has calling out, for them, become more intrinsic to lessons than even listening? Actually, come to think of it, have they subconsciously stopped listening because they're so busy calling out?

'Excellent. Thanks for reflecting on that. We've got some situations in which this is happening. All we've got to do now is to work out why ...'

Bearing in mind that Miss Marple gets what feels like weeks, you have some leeway on this one. Exploring emotions, self-awareness, blink-of-an-eye decision-making is obviously not something you can shortcut. However, having tunnelled deep enough to confirm that calling out happens and in which situations, you'll be much closer to finding out why. So, as with other questions, prod, nudge, cajole, back off when you sense you need to, listen, don't judge, learn. If it takes a few weeks, so be it. A few months, the same. My guess is that the can of worms you'll be starting to open contains opportunities for improving not just the act of your student calling out, unhelpfully, in class, but their overall conduct and contentment at school.

DO I PUT MY BEST EFFORT INTO MY SCHOOLWORK?

I guess not, particularly if all of the above is going pear-shaped too. Who would? You can't pay attention, you've stopped listening to your teachers (certainly when they're so negative all the time), you behave like you're a decade younger than you are and you spend so much time calling out, you've started to sound more like a city trader than a school pupil. Come to think of it, maybe that's your problem – you're a stockbroker trapped in a primary school pupil's clothing. Bit juvenile, maybe, but we can't let youth be wasted on the young yet again. Thanks for all this teaching stuff, but I'm off to put my best effort into flogging some stocks.

Effort is a serious buzzword at schools – used to praise, to encourage and, of course, to criticise. I can hear the one-liner now: 'Joshua Francis, if you put as much effort into your schoolwork as you do distracting others, you'd be top of the class by now.' It feels as lame an if-clause as it is tempting to use, but maybe there is something in this tired rebuke. How is it that a pupil, seemingly void of the effort gene, can so doggedly wear a teacher down with such fantastic attention to making everyone else's life a complete misery? Emotions aside, there's great spirit in there. Wonderful tenacity. An eye for the prize. Dedication. Application. Uncompromising focus. Imagine what that would look like applied to a different purpose.

I listened to football pundit Ian Wright recently, emotionally teeing up his favourite music for an imaginary desert island, recounting how being made milk monitor at school turned his view of himself on its head, because finally his energies were being channelled into something productive and mildly honourable.[5] Alright, he was (presumably) only collecting and handing out little bottles of full fat cow's milk to his classmates. But as I understand it, with this one simple job he felt he had been given a purpose, something to live up to, a focus that had all sorts of good rewards at the end of it – praise, self-esteem, work ethic, feeling generous, teacher relationship and maybe even an extra bottle of milk or two at the end of it.

This was a tonic for a little boy with a difficult life, whose childhood, it would seem, was shrouded in negativity, conflict and ill-management. How many of those pupils walk through our school gates every day? How many are so down on their lives and their luck that making the effort to do their schoolwork – however much, deep down, they would like to try – is really quite beyond them? A good many, I would guess. A good many.

So, if this is your pupil's need, start small. Start milk monitor. And if one of Margaret Thatcher's legacies as education secretary lives on, and there's no more milk to be had, start book collector. Or board wiper. Or office runner. Or pen hander-outer. Or for older kids, maybe rubbish collector. Or plastics monitor. Or open day parents taker-rounder. Or parents' evening tea-maker. Or anything in fact, anything with that wonderful -er suffix that means you've become something in life. You are the noun that proves the verb. You do something. And it's recognised with a title. You may not have a badge or a salary or pay national insurance or income tax, and you may not get your photo taken and put on a noticeboard, or given a company car or car allowance, and you may not receive a knighthood or a CBE or whatever you get for services to your profession, but what you do get is a little bit of recognition – a little something that says someone else in

---

5   *Desert Island Discs* with former Arsenal striker Ian Wright, *BBC Radio 4* (16 February 2020). Available at: https://www.bbc.co.uk/programmes/m000fdxw.

the world, maybe even two people, values you and recognises you for what you do. And do you know what, that feels good sometimes. That feels really good.

Just maybe when your pupil next sits down in that teacher's classroom, instead of chucking their rubber or banging on their desk, they might just listen. And once they've listened, they might also work. And, chances are, there will be effort going into that work. You don't need me to explain the potential of the dynamic between teacher and pupil; it's just how it is.

All of that said, your pupil might not be the younger Ian Wright. Or anything like him. Their home life might be relatively serene, their emotions intact and their knowledge base considerable. Or just one or two of those scenarios. But for some reason they just won't bite the bullet and work. We assign certain adjectives to such young people – we call them lazy or spoilt or indulged, for example. We call them work-shy or apathetic. All or some of which may have truth in them, but how often do we ask not just *why* but *what* can they and I do about it? I'm their teacher. Their teaching assistant. Their head of year. I'm the volunteer they chat to in the dining hall. Their favourite dinner lady. The caretaker who lives both definitions of his job title. I'm the head, the deputy, the acting assistant to the assistant deputy to the head. Whoever you are, whatever job title has been assigned to you, you can ask that question – of yourself and of them.

I guarantee that, given time – and let's face it, given love – you'll find some answers that, even if only partly, answer the question of what this particular pupil can do to meet their own needs to put their best effort into their school work. If you've read this far, I suspect – notwithstanding time and the right support around you – you are the person who can help.

DO I PUT MY BEST EFFORT INTO MY HOMEWORK?

Running a breakfast homework club has taught me a few things. Other than the fact that sugar-laden breakfast bars are way cheaper to provide than apples.

I already knew the lead balloon that asks teenagers to get up even earlier than normal, although I've been surprised at how alert they are once they are in school early. I had some idea that they might sometimes struggle with user names and passwords for online homework sites, although I'd not realised to what extent. And, of course, I had the impression that homework is generally there to be done with rather than slaved over. However, I'd forgotten just how pitifully a piece of work can be tackled sometimes, with the pupil perpetrator seemingly oblivious to its lack of depth, content, legibility, name, title, date, you name it. Literally, a two-minute scrawl on a random piece of ripped paper can satisfy some of our less-discerning clients.

'Is that how you're going to hand it in?'

'Yeah, that's how I always hand it in.'

'Do you think it might be missing a little care?'

'Hmm ... no, not really.'

'OK. Let me introduce you to a few simple basics that will transform your work ...'

With this passport question, you're trying to get to a place whereby the pupil takes on the adage that if a job's worth doing, it's worth doing properly. Getting it done is OK, but that's what you do when you take the rubbish out or clear the table. No frills, just needs to be done. Whereas homework, you would have them understand, is more akin to say, cleaning your own car: you can get it done but you're not going to be very proud driving around in it afterwards, with smears on the windows, half-cleaned wheel hubs and a fly-spattered number plate.

Homework (as mentioned in Chapter 5), so your message goes, can be a means to a consolidated, deeper learning which develops skills and makes classroom learning more accessible: 'What about the pride of handing in some-thing over which you've worked really hard? Ever tasted that? No, OK, let's do a tasting. Show me your homework list ...'

While I'd say I'm firmly in the camp of life being too short for too much homework, the evidence is out there that, in moderation and well-targeted, it works. For example, researchers in a 2014 Department for Education-funded study of pupils aged 3–16 found quite unequivocally that time spent on homework 'on a typical school night' was a 'strong positive predictor of academic attainment in Year 9 and progress between KS2 and KS3'. Perhaps unsurpris-ingly, it also proved to be the case at Key Stage 4. For those doing two to three hours of work a night, 'the relationship between time spent on homework and academic out-comes showed a broadly linear pattern'.[6]

So, if you want a simple equation, it would appear that P (pupil) + H (homework) + E (effort) = G (grades). But if you just want a few bullets on how to inspire a habit that evolves from 'What homework?' to 'Done it – happy now?'

---

6   Department for Education, *Influences on Students' GCSE Attainment and Progress at Age 16: Effective Pre-school, Primary & Secondary Education Project (EPPSE)*. Research Report (September 2014), p. 74. Available at: https://assets.publishing. service.gov.uk/government/uploads/system/uploads/attachment_data/file/ 373286/RR352_-_Influences_on_Students_GCSE_Attainment_and_Progress_at_ Age_16.pdf.

to 'Did you read and mark my homework, miss?', these might be of use:

- Encourage pupils to go to homework clubs before (breakfast is a great little enticer) or after school.

- Offer your own help during passport sessions – it might be just the leg-up they need.

- Enlist the support of parents, carers and siblings where possible – their encouragement, inducement and engagement have been behind many a homework powerhouse.

- Help children to create a routine – agree a set day, set time and set place.

- Speak to teachers if the work doesn't seem pitched at the right level for your pupil.

- Check and review the learning with the pupil afterwards.

A few homework success stories early on could just pave the way for your pupil to gain the confidence and the belief that it might just be worth putting their best effort into their homework.

CHEYENNE (CONTINUED)

What is my need in attitude to learning?

'Put more effort into my homework.'

What I can do to meet this need:

'Work thoroughly on homework and make it neat. Keep attending homework club and ask sir to nag me to work better. Tell mum when I get commendations for homework.'

My feelings about my efforts to meet my needs:

Week 1: 'I feel greatfull for homework club.'

Week 2: 'Need to work harder.'

Week 3: 'I'm working hard in homework club and will keep it up.'

Week 4: 'I worked thoroughly on my maths homework and some others.'

Needs partly met ✓

DO I CHECK MY WORK THOROUGHLY WHEN I FINISH TASKS?

About a year ago, I started talking to certain subject teachers I knew to ask to what extent they marked work for accurate punctuation. Did a history essay need to be well punctuated, with capital letters for names of battles and generals? Should 'U-shaped valley' have not just a capital letter but a hyphen too? Would two identical pieces of writing in RE – except for one's attention to, and one's neglect for, punctuation – gain significantly different marks?

What I think I understood was that 'Yes, we mark for it, and, yes, it's on the examiner's mark scheme, and, yes, it's still important,' but also that 'Actually, well, you can't mark everything, and it's not the be-and-end-all, and content is far more important, after all, so you know what, at a glance, if there's some punctuation dotted around the place (alongside some decent spelling and grammar), I'll give them more extra SPaG marks, and if there's not much in the way of dots and caps, I'll give them fewer.' In short, it's an impression thing, not a scientific one.

The more I looked into it, the more I became convinced that perfecting your punctuation – outside the parameters of English language exams – just isn't that big a deal any more. So get over it, granddad. Comma schmomma. Full stops when I fancy; brackets my arse. I can work with that, I thought. When you've still got a hanky in one pocket, a Nokia in the other and you're sporting a jumper from the 1990s, it's not a great leap to think that you might be out of touch on the hallmarks of acceptable writing too.

However, whatever the state of the un- or ill-punctuated piece, the one thing you really can't do without – whether it's a Year 8 science experiment write-up, an email to the taxman or your will – is your writing making sense. Ideally first time. But at least second. No one's going to bother with a third. Your teacher, the taxman, your executor will all have given up by then – there are plenty more children, self-employers, dead people where you came from.

And before you ask, yes, commas can be vital in not misinterpreting and exclamation and question marks should only be deployed alone, and for the right reasons, and yes, to me, good punctuation is important and should be taught. But you can't have everything – especially if a good many students and teachers are voting with their feet on this one.

In such a climate, it feels more pressing, therefore, that missing words are inserted, poor wording is reworded and, as a minimal nod to punctuation, full stops are used to break up those interminably long sentences – you know, the ones by the end of which you've lost the will to live, let alone have any idea what the writer's on about.

If their writing makes sense, your student at least has a chance. So, get this target – I mean need – on their agenda if the work your student produces, unchecked, is what you or they (or their taxman) might describe as ill-written or confusing because this need is their need. Additionally, of course, instil in them that checking involves accuracy of content, which involves research and double-checking of facts and figures, thoughts and assertions. Which isn't just a good lesson for lessons, but not a bad lesson for life either.

So, the how is firstly about care and then it's about habit. Find out why the care has slipped or was never there; what need in your student isn't being met for them to want or feel able to care; how they, through you or other key adults, can influence how that need is met; and then, at your conversation's most positive moment, hit them with a new habit: five minutes of checking at the end of every piece of homework. Or even at the end of just one. Per week. Lower or heighten the bar according to your judgement of the depth of need.

'Never checked a piece of work in my life, sir.'

'OK, let's start small then.'

It's important to add that your student may have barriers to checking their work thoroughly – to understanding whether their work makes sense or is accurate, however long they slave over it. These barriers may be significant; just because something is obvious to us, doesn't mean it is so to them. Looking over a selection of pieces of work with them will give you some insight into this. But, as always, check with teachers, tutors, SEN staff and other interested parties. It might be that your student is dyslexic.

As with ADHD, as any experiencer knows, dyslexia – and the diagnosis of it – comes with a health warning: others may think it bogus. But your 12-point education plan – for your student, your colleagues and yourself (derived primarily from the teaching of our friends at www.understood. org, including literacy expert Margie B. Gillis) – goes something like this:

1 Dyslexia is a learning difficulty in reading.

2 There are differences in the function of the brain between people who have dyslexia and those who don't.

3 It can affect absolutely anyone.

4 People with dyslexia have trouble decoding words (matching letters to sounds).

5 They can also struggle to recognise the sounds in words (phonemic awareness).

6 They don't (any more than anyone else) have less willpower. Or less intelligence. Or impaired vision. See number 2 – their brain processes things differently.

7 It can take them a long time to read and understand a written piece – way longer than someone without dyslexia; the same goes for writing it.

8 Letters such as b and d, and p and q, are often mixed up, and good spelling is extremely difficult to master.

9 They can struggle to express feelings appropriately.

10 They sometimes miss social cues, such as facial expressions and body language.

11 Given effective strategies, good support and strong resilience, children and adults can draw on other parts of the brain to learn to read and spell well.

12 There's a good chance that a person's dyslexia is hereditary – it's not uncommon for siblings and parents to be dyslexic too.[7]

Once identified (use the usual channels to solicit help in diagnosing), number 11 in this list is clearly the most significant. Despite the innately different processing of a dyslexic child's brain, strategies exist which will help your student to conquer reading – so their brain learns to process in a way that aids, rather than obstructs, reading – and with it, the accompanying social and emotional difficulties. These strategies don't cure them – they don't make them non-dyslexic. But they do enable them to get round the problem, like glasses for sight issues. Just don't underestimate how tirelessly someone with dyslexia has to work – even with strategies and good support – to overcome this barrier. It's one thing wearing a pair of spectacles; it's another trying to rewire your own brain.

RYAN

What is my need in attitude to learning?

'Check my work thoroughly when I finish tasks.'

What I can do to meet this need:

'Try and go through homework slowly. Start with English. I will check with me first and then my mum and dad. Ask perants to remind me.'

---

7 See https://www.understood.org/en/learning-thinking-differences/child-learning-disabilities/dyslexia/what-is-dyslexia#Dyslexia_Signs_and_Symptoms, https://www.understood.org/en/learning-thinking-differences/child-learning-disabilities/dyslexia/ways-dyslexia-can-affect-social-skills and https://www.understood.org/en/learning-thinking-differences/child-learning-disabilities/dyslexia/skills-that-can-be-affected-by-dyslexia?.

My feelings about my efforts to meet my needs:

Week 1: 'I'm normaly more intrested in my phone and going on YouTube insted of cheking homework.'

Week 2: 'Only sciming at the moment. Perants telling me to spend five mins checking.'

Week 3: 'Some time's go through the book not all time.'

Week 4: 'It is helping.'

Needs partly met ✓

TAYLOR

What is my need in attitude to learning?

'Check my work thoroughly.'

What I can do to meet this need:

'Finish homework five minutes early and spend it checking work. Ask parents to remind me. Check classwork when teacher gives time to check.'

My feelings about my efforts to meet my needs:

Week 1: 'I was off sick all week.'

Week 2: 'I did OK. Not much homework checking but did classwork.'

Week 3: 'No opportunity to check in lessons. Can only remember checking one piece of homework. Happy I checked it. Will try and check more.'

Week 4: 'Haven't checked any work – homework or schoolwork. I feel disappointed.'

Needs not met ✓

DO I ASK FOR HELP WHEN I'M STUCK?

'I'd rather eat the contents of my own pencil case. Starting with the compass.'

What is it about asking for help that can be so painful? So degrading? So glutes-tensingly uncomfortable? How is it that some pupils can throw up their hands with aplomb, barely a break between question and answer, and others would rather lose circulation in their hands than take them out from under their hamstrings?

Why is it that it is so difficult sometimes to admit that you can't do something? That you don't understand it? That it doesn't make sense to you? That however hard you try to squeeze the information into your stubborn brain, it just won't go in? Is it pride? Embarrassment? A sign of weakness? Failure? Or a potent mix of all four? Or maybe it's just a habit that you either get yourself into or slowly prevent yourself from ever developing? Whichever which way, if it ain't happening, it's worth addressing.

And, of course, we're not talking about turning children into serial help-seekers here, among whose number I can previously count myself. A boss in an old job used to have a brilliant retort for my incessant questions about this, that and everything: 'Well, you tell me.' No, we're trying to help the pupil who, for whatever reason, doesn't know, who has tried but can't work it out, but also who, at all costs, won't ask. Not even Siri.

Look into the problem together by encouraging your pupil to talk about what it is that goes through their mind, what emotions they feel, when they've tried and are still stuck but don't want to ask. The answers to these questions are their needs. The need to feel less stupid, less humiliated, less powerless, less inferior.

And when you've arrived at the need, push them to think about what *they* can do to meet it. Does it involve more work? Or a strategy to develop more self-confidence? Or even more humility? Does it involve them asking you to ask someone else if they can help bridge this need in some way? A teacher who comes over quietly to assist, maybe once a lesson, to build the rapport, to help form the habit. And then the next week does the same. But in the third week, looks for a nod from the pupil to come over, please. And then a coy hand up. And then a coy one with words. And then, well, who knows after then. They might just have broken the back of it. Small steps, though, and ones that can be retrodden should things move too fast or without initial success.

MERIEM

What is my need in attitude to learning?

'To ask for help when I'm stuck.'

What I can do to meet this need:

'Put my hand up or stand up and go and ask for help instead of chatting to my friend.'

My feelings about my efforts to meet my needs:

Week 1: 'I asked for help in English and it helped me complete the work.'

Week 2: 'I've tried in French but the teacher didn't hear.'

Week 3: 'I've been asking for help in maths and it's helping.'

Week 4: 'It's working.'

Needs met ✓

AM I COMFORTABLE MAKING MISTAKES?

This question very much ties into the last one. I'm sure you recognise the situation: you're so scared of Layla's reaction to your assertion, however delicately put, that she's wrong, that you daren't say it. Madly racking your brain to find a way to tell this child that somehow they're not wrong, even when in fact they are. Or a halfway house to praise just something in Layla's claim that Paris is most definitely the capital of Spain.

'Well, it is a capital of somewhere – very good ... and that somewhere isn't altogether far from Spain ... they share a border in fact – brilliant! I can see exactly where you're coming from there.'

'Is it right then, sir?'

'It very nearly is, yes.'

'So it's wrong.'

'A little bit, yes.'

And with that final reluctant yes, which confirms an ultimately unthinkable no, Layla is gone. The sarcasm comes flying out, face turns puce, body language turns feral, book is slammed shut, pen is disposed of and nothing but nothing can stop another lesson, for Layla and her neighbours at least, being consigned to the waste bin of school lessons.

How to help a child, or adult in fact, feel more comfortable making mistakes is a tall order. You, or their teachers, can have as rule number 3 of the Official Class Rules, 'Be comfortable making mistakes', you can have 20-foot posters of inspirational quotes stating that 'Anyone who has never made a mistake has never tried anything new' and 'Your best teacher is your last mistake' and 'Experiment, fail, learn, repeat'. You can tirelessly praise effort and you can skew more of your questioning towards a more Thunk style of questioning[8] – those without yes or no answers, only opinion, conjecture and thought-sharing. But, ultimately, if none of that succeeds, you're probably going to have to have the emotions chat referred to in the previous answer.

Dig around, see what you come up with (together), use your emotional literacy (together) and put in place some plans to meet needs (together), ideally ones designed to break down a few barriers. The education system, and indeed society, is very good at raising its protégés to think that all that matters is whether you're right or wrong. Disabusing a child of this inaccuracy is your not inconsiderable task.

---

8   See I. Gilbert, *The Little Book of Thunks: 260 Questions to Make Your Brain Go Ouch!* (Carmarthen: Crown House Publishing, 2007).

AM I POLITE TO ALL STAFF AT SCHOOL?

You know how without fuel a car can't function? And the same without wheels? But without air con it's less pleasant a ride but the car still goes? So too, perhaps, the child without politeness. I mean, it's not going to change their grades, is it? You can get a 9 without saying please or thank you or excuse me. And it's not like they're at school for brownie points. So, despite the comfier ride to the exams hall, why be polite?

Working with children has taught me a lesson or two. Not that politeness isn't important, but that politeness isn't an automatic right. None of us can necessarily expect another person to be polite just because we'd like them to be. Cards on the table: I'm one of those people who thinks it's important to be polite. And I'm also one of those teachers who has called pupils rude for not being so. But I think I might have missed something.

Firstly, not all families are polite. In fact, let's face it, it's how many of us function, the more familiar we become with one another. It may be born of contempt in some cases or comfort in others, but it is sometimes how we grow to be.

Secondly, even if you think your pupil isn't being polite, he or she may not be aware of it – even if you can't believe that can possibly be so. Not everyone believes that the only way to ask for something is with a please and to be thankful for something is with a thank you – let alone to be sorry for something is with a sorry. My wife would rather put a match to her shoe collection. Or book us a holiday. Anything but that five-letter grovel.

And thirdly, in conflict or in stress, an omission of politeness is obviously one of those behaviours that is trying to communicate a message – that 'I don't like you,' that 'I don't like what you've told me,' that 'I don't like the way you spoke to me or how you did it in public' or even that 'However beautifully you just expressed yourself, or however justified you were in talking to me in the way you just did, I am not in a very good place right now and I really, really don't feel like being polite to you just because you think it's important. Have I made myself clear ... er, miss?'

So why ask the question? Because, I guess, that just because something can't necessarily be expected, doesn't mean it's not a good rule of thumb. The young people who get on at school know that it helps to curry favour. They know it feels good to bestow politeness on others and to have that politeness returned. They know it's a power with a force that can break down many barriers – that a well-timed, well-meaning sorry can take the heat out of a situation, the wind out of a tirade, the detention out of a punishment. They know that it can show respect to staff whose income, if not whose work, is less than others'. They know it shows gratitude to those people who give their time, without remuneration, to support the school. They know that however they use it, it works, in any number of ways, for the good of both them and of others.

So, encourage politeness – not because it's a custom but because it helps. And if your pupil is a long way from feeling the self-respect and inner warmth that it sometimes takes to feel thankful or grateful or courteous or, indeed, sorry, then that is most clearly their need and there is no better starting point than that: 'So, tell me, how are we going to get you to like and feel better about yourself a bit more?'

DO I HELP OTHERS
WITH THEIR LEARNING?

It takes a certain confidence to get up from your desk, walk over to someone else's and start helping them with their learning. Especially if the teacher didn't sanction it or the other student didn't ask for it. A little bit full of yourself, in fact.

But hopefully that's not what we're getting at here. Helping others – whatever form it takes – generates self-esteem; of that we are all innately aware. Your student should have access to that feeling, just like everyone else. If they can do so in the arena of their learning, even better.

The reason being, as you may have learned during teacher training, is that, when you teach something to someone else, you consolidate your own understanding of it. To a significant degree. In fact, in the Peak Performance Center's Learning Pyramid, it is far and away the best method of learning because it results in 90% learner recall. By contrast, you'll be surprised to hear, being lectured leads to just 5% learner recall (universities, take note) and reading 10%.[9] Now, these figures depend not just on the laboratory in which they were conducted, but also on the type of learner, so we are well advised to take them not so much at face value but as a general guide.

All of that said, you may have on your hands a student who doesn't feel confident in a good many areas of their learning, and the last thing they would like to do is start teaching someone else something they don't really

9   The Learning Pyramid was researched and created by the National Training Laboratories in the United States: see J. Kelly, The learning pyramid, *Peak Performance Center* (September 2012). Available at: https://thepeakperformance center.com/educational-learning/learning/principles-of-learning/learning-pyramid.

understand themselves. No problem. But I challenge you both to find the one area, at least, where they do have expertise over others or even just one other. Whether it is in sport or music or maths or the arts, you can pretty much guarantee that every student has a core strength. And even if that core strength isn't as strong as 28 other young learners in their class, so long as there is one student who could benefit from their extra knowledge, time and explanation, then you have yourself a tutor–pupil relationship.

If this is the area that your student wishes to pursue, then between you, move heaven and earth to make it happen. Discussions with teachers or just between students – the times we've all seen impromptu peer tutoring in the library, the corridor, outside and inside the classroom – will help to open up opportunities for this key interaction to take place.

Not everyone is a born teacher, of course. Not even some teachers. So, in the 'What I can do to meet this need' section, you will be looking to share a few tips to support this young educator. You know, how to impart without condescending, to explain without boring, to lead without telling.

Helping others with their learning is, without question, the hallmark not just of a competent student; it is also the hallmark of a kind, empathic one – and we surely need both if we are to give our children as rounded an education as we can.

CODY

What is my need in attitude to learning?

'Help others.'

What I can do to meet this need:

'Help people get to the answers when I have finished. Help them but dont tell them. Try it in all of my subjects.'

My feelings about my efforts to meet my needs:

Week 1: 'I havent started because I havent finished early.'

Week 2: 'Started working better with others. Trying to put up with it.'

Week 3: 'Worked with Daisy in RE to complete the work.'

Week 4: 'Good group work in drama. I help people more.'

Needs met ✓

CHAPTER 7
SETTING

THE CLASSROOM

I have fond memories of the classroom, although I also have the not-so-fond ones. I call them memories because I've not taught in normal 30-something classes for six years now. I call it the classroom because what I teach in now can't really be referred to as such. It's more of an en suite without the bath, sink or loo – and in their place, a couple of kids delighted to be missing history.

I say I have fond memories because the classroom – the real one you all teach, assist or observe in – feels like a proper amphitheatre. Exposed on all sides, even from the glaringly white whiteboard, you really have to perform in that arena to earn your keep. And it is something about the rare occasions when you really get a class fired up and they really respond to your teaching – enjoying themselves *and* working hard all at the same time – that you can live off for months, somewhat conveniently.

And then there are the much commoner occasions when it just isn't working and everything you touch turns a rusty shade of copper. Kids shouting, books missing, eyes rolling, teacher drowning; all of you crawling your way to the end of what you might generously have called your lesson. I guess that is why it feels like an amphitheatre – sink or swim, you are going to have to take whatever it throws back at you.

I mention both of these types of room – your proper teaching one and my executive en suite version – because it's important that we acknowledge the elephant who can't fit into either of them: that a teacher who has more white-board pens than he does pupils has the temerity to think that what happens in his luxury yacht of a room is some-how transferrable to your overcrowded ferry. In short, that using the passport with two pupils will be just as simple and as effective as with 30.

Just so we're clear, that is not what I'm saying. You can't do this stuff with full classes – trust me, I've tried. And I wasn't even the real teacher. All I had to do was manage the pass-ports. I could barely manage the signatures next to the dates that signified pupils had even sat in front of one; I had no idea if half of them had even read or responded to them.

I shouldn't say you can't do this with full classes. What I should really say is you can't expect to, with any degree of depth – unless you are one of those seriously impressive juggle-everything type of teacher. But what you can do is to try it out in one of the following settings, should your school or line manager free you up to do so.

ONE-TO-ONE

For: any staff who can afford up to an hour a week for five weeks

Especially: intervention and nurture teachers, mentors, teaching assistants and learning support assistants, and teachers with an abnormally light workload (one must exist somewhere)

Like me, even if just for a five-week period to begin with, you may be able to get yourself up to an hour's slot in which to get really stuck into the passport's nitty-gritty with your chosen pupil. Like Noah, you can invite guests in twos, but one is preferable – these are pupils who will lap up your undivided attention, even if it is a little difficult to tell to begin with.

A quiet room works for the staff–pupil pairing who are familiar with each other – assuming you both feel comfortable and are able to have an open door – and for those who aren't, a more public but still quiet place such as the school library would be a good venue. It's as well to discuss this first with your pupil; in a library, you can talk discreetly but, even then, not everyone will wish to air their school linen there.

As outlined in Chapter 3, you will have prepared your pupil's passport and highlighter in advance, so all they have to do in this first week, not dissimilar to going on *Pointless*, is turn up and answer the questions. With introspection and a good discussion. But no cash jackpot.

Remember that this is their passport, as personalised for them by you. You know this young person best, their little quirks and foibles, so feel free to change or adapt questions however you see fit. In particular, you will need to decide if you would like the movable feast section – at the top right of the passport – to be about literacy (as in Figure 1 on pages 22–25), about reading (see Figure 2) or about any other school area you choose, from RE (see Figure 3) or geography to school playground or lunch hall behaviour. Whether your questions are about key words or key skills learning, about returning your dinner tray and thanking staff for lunch, or perhaps about not using Year 7s as human footballs during breaktime, they must have your chosen pupil in mind.

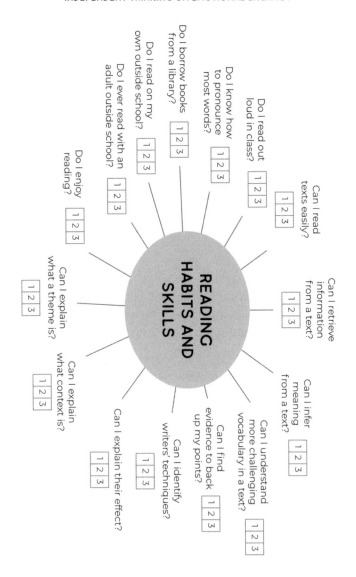

FIGURE 2. READING PASSPORT

Note: Colour copies of the passport can be downloaded for free from:
https://www.crownhouse.co.uk/featured/emotional-literacy.

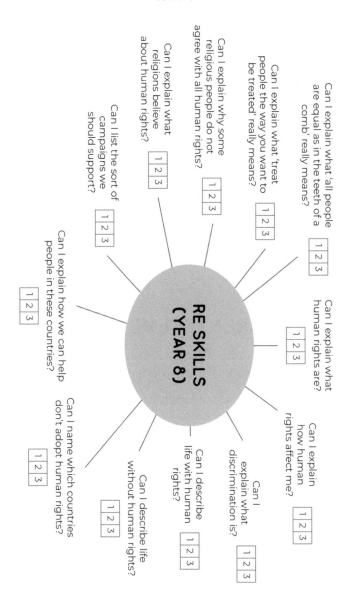

Can I explain what 'all people are equal as in the teeth of a comb' really means?

[1] [2] [3]

Can I explain what 'treat people the way you want to be treated' really means?

[1] [2] [3]

Can I explain why some religious people do not agree with all human rights?

[1] [2] [3]

Can I explain what religions believe about human rights?

[1] [2] [3]

Can I list the sort of campaigns we should support?

[1] [2] [3]

Can I explain how we can help people in these countries?

[1] [2] [3]

RE SKILLS (YEAR 8)

Can I explain what human rights are?

[1] [2] [3]

Can I explain how human rights affect me?

[1] [2] [3]

Can I explain what discrimination is?

[1] [2] [3]

Can I describe life with human rights?

[1] [2] [3]

Can I describe life without human rights?

[1] [2] [3]

Can I name which countries don't adopt human rights?

[1] [2] [3]

FIGURE 3. RE PASSPORT

Note: Colour copies of the passport can be downloaded for free from: https://www.crownhouse.co.uk/featured/emotional-literacy.

A word of warning: your pupil may seem distinctly under-whelmed or caught in headlights to begin with. That's not unheard of. Some won't be used to this sort of question-ing; many won't be used to this sort of attention. So, as with green pen marking (when pupils are tasked with improving their own work), in order to avoid the lip-service treatment, children need to be guided and taught how to discuss, respond, reflect and assess – in some detail. Take your time and give them space; their first week's work may just need a part 2 next time around.

Refer back to Chapter 3 for your next steps and don't be afraid, on successful completion of four weeks of reflec-tion, to initiate a second passport based on their next needs in a week, month or even a term's time.

PARENTS' EVENING

For: those who have or support a form

Especially: form tutors wanting to make more of a difference

You're going to need help on this one, so don't start haring down the aisles to hand out passports before you've even taken the register – like I once did. You might find it's filled in and returned before you've even asked Abi Adams if she's here. Actually, I'm being disingenuous: there were highs and even successes, but there were also kids for whom the passport meant about as much as a paper place mat. For which, if anyone is interested, I'm happy to take orders.

Why? Well, because, as you will have been saying to your-self since the start, this thing can't be achieved in anything like the sort of depth it needs in big groups. I mean, you could save one form period a week to ask the whole class, as one, whether they behave in lessons, and they could, as one, reply, 'Are you kidding us, miss?' and you could retort, 'Well, what are you going to do about it then, 9MR?' and they could reply all together and in ascending volume, 'Start behaving like Year 9s and not under 9s, miss,' and you could laugh and say, 'I couldn't agree more, collective form – so let's see you do it,' and they could chant in unison, 'Oh no, we couldn't,' and you could counter that, 'Oh yes, they could,' and that could go on until the bell and (in my head at least) it would be enormous fun and provide great slapstick and bonding, but it wouldn't leave you any the wiser come parents' evening.

So, how to use the passport as preparation for the night of the parent? My suggestion is to choose a few students who you know are slipping under the radar and a few who most certainly aren't – you know, in ways that everyone knows about but few are enjoying. Or just choose one from each subset. Or even just one. You'll barely have time to wee between lessons if you're anything like a normal form tutor, so start small.

Once you've got your charge or charges, earmark time – at least five weeks in advance of parents' evening – to meet them for their first session. Two (who complement) at a time is fine: while one talks, the other can write. Yes, you're going to need to eat into your own schedule but, no, it won't be a waste of time. Far from it – come parents' evening, they will be the students about whom you most want to talk because you will have most to say.

Name: .... Date: ....

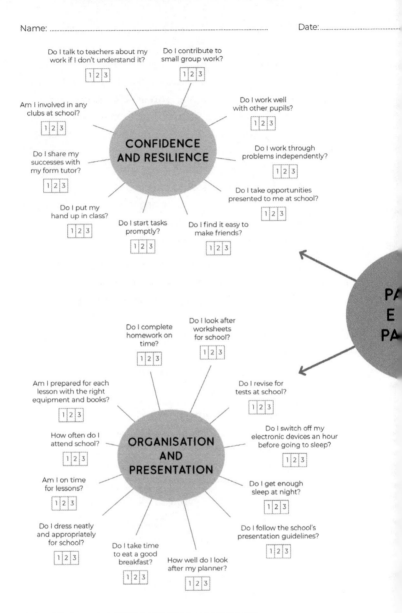

FIGURE 4. PARENTS' EVENING PASSPORT

Note: Colour copies of the passport can be downloaded for free from:
https://www.crownhouse.co.uk/featured/emotional-literacy.

Form: ....

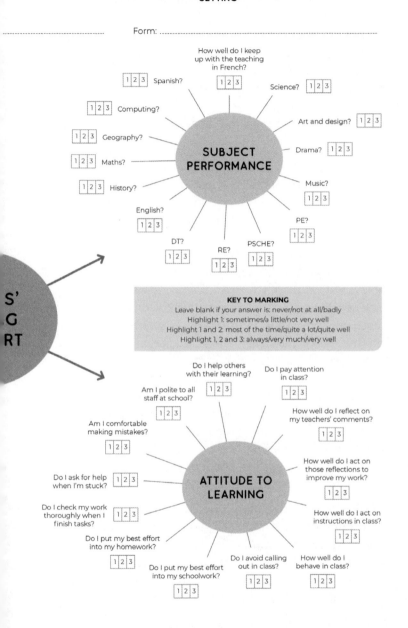

How well do I keep up with the teaching in French? 1 2 3

Spanish? 1 2 3

Science? 1 2 3

Computing? 1 2 3

Art and design? 1 2 3

Geography? 1 2 3

Drama? 1 2 3

Maths? 1 2 3

History? 1 2 3

Music? 1 2 3

English? 1 2 3

PE? 1 2 3

DT? 1 2 3

RE? 1 2 3

PSCHE? 1 2 3

SUBJECT PERFORMANCE

S' G RT

KEY TO MARKING
Leave blank if your answer is: never/not at all/badly
Highlight 1: sometimes/a little/not very well
Highlight 1 and 2: most of the time/quite a lot/quite well
Highlight 1, 2 and 3: always/very much/very well

Do I help others with their learning? 1 2 3

Do I pay attention in class? 1 2 3

Am I polite to all staff at school? 1 2 3

How well do I reflect on my teachers' comments? 1 2 3

Am I comfortable making mistakes? 1 2 3

How well do I act on those reflections to improve my work? 1 2 3

Do I ask for help when I'm stuck? 1 2 3

ATTITUDE TO LEARNING

How well do I act on instructions in class? 1 2 3

Do I check my work thoroughly when I finish tasks? 1 2 3

Do I put my best effort into my homework? 1 2 3

Do I put my best effort into my schoolwork? 1 2 3

Do I avoid calling out in class? 1 2 3

How well do I behave in class? 1 2 3

Go through the passport as outlined in Chapter 3, making sure to agree needs and how to meet them by the end of the first session. Absolutely make sure to print out coloured stickers with needs emblazoned across them and be sure they are duly stuck at the front of their planners. Keep a copy for your own planner – they are your weaponry at parents' evening.

You'll notice that the *subject performance* section in Figure 4 asks students how well they keep up with the teaching in each subject. Let their answers serve as a guide, but obviously let subject teachers be the final arbiters – the comparison will certainly be of interest. Of more pertinence, however, are the other three sections. For both student and teacher to be able to talk knowledgably about that student's efforts to work through problems independently; to complete each, most or some subject teachers' homework on time; and to avoid calling out in maths, French or Ancient Greek studies will, I can all but guarantee you, overlap with some of their subject teachers' own targets for them: Mr Adesanya's pleas to concentrate more, Miss Dunn's to chat less, Mrs Costa's request for a well-completed piece of homework, just one of these days, if you don't mind, please. You'll link your student's work on their passport needs with their teacher's targets for their subjects, and, hey presto, a funny sort of accidentally deliberate joined-up working will be in action.

But why stop there? Permit me a little pipe dream here. Just imagine a room full of students and parents doing their utmost to ensure a regular good breakfast before school, but not entirely sure how, having access to a dietician or two sprinkled around the parents' evening sidelines to offer tips on nutrition and food economy.

Imagine too those trying to get enough rest at night, after months or years of struggle, with access to a row of pyjamaed sleep consultants (they exist, I promise you – without the pyjamas, at least) at the back of the hall. Or those with the full gamut of tricky parenting questions being able to pick the brains of educators like Victoria Prooday from Chapter 5. Or those struggling with the inordinate pressures of a child or children with obsessive-compulsive disorder, autism or dyspraxia having access to a clinically trained professional. That's not to say that SEN teams don't have great knowledge, insight and empathy – their work in school is a lifeline to these children, plenty with great expertise – but, in general, can we expect them to have the deeper understanding and strategies of a clinician?

For too long now, teachers at tables at parents' evenings – barely visible beneath the queues of report-clutching parents – and the staff who work alongside them have been trying to be jacks of all trades, answering all manner of really important and difficult questions.

Teachers should be talking about teaching and learning – and all that comprises the pedagogical journey, such as self-motivating, organising and revising. They should be igniting the fuses of those mini knowledge rockets in front of them. Yes, as form tutors, they are there to guide and provide pastoral care, but that is the job that got thrown in with the main one – it is not their specialism and, more importantly, it is not what they are given time to do.

Nurture and care for 30-odd children, simultaneously, in 20-odd minutes per day, when there is also the register to take? And school notices and initiatives to deliver? And assembly to go to? And lateness and absence to contend with? Are you kidding me?

By all means, let those who can make the time use in-itiatives like the passport to open up debate, listen and offer kindness, and provide common-sense solutions to long-standing problems. But for the stuff that is more complex and specialised, surely it's not beyond the wit and budget of education to team up with professionals of industry, lifestyle, health and social care to support students who need both an education *and* the tailored personal support which will make viable that education in the first place? And to provide that at parents' evenings when the issues arise and need answering? Surely it isn't?

But, until then, don't despair because following your passport work, you and your student have just had a proper parents' evening conversation with their parents or carers. A conversation based on your student's very personal efforts to meet their very personal needs. They have shown themselves willing to self-reflect and engage. However little they or you might feel they have progressed in five or so weeks, they are involved and trying. And even if they're not trying, they are aware of their lack of effort and of some of the reasons that may lay behind it. And they can talk about it with a degree of self-knowledge – rather than cringe into their chair while the surrounding adults shake their heads and stare daggers at them. It might not sound like it, but I can assure you that is progress.

You can't move mountains, however. You can't beat the system – not just yet, anyway. You're only impacting one student out of your whole class, maybe two. But that may be one needy student more than last parents' evening. And who knows what that attention and support might do for the educational and, in turn, life chances of that particular child? Or how the practice might spread from one in your class to one in a few others? It's got to be worth a try.

DETENTION

For: any staff who can free themselves up for one session a week for five weeks

Especially: head teachers, deputy heads, assistant heads, heads of year/department, intervention and nurture teachers, teaching assistants, learning support assistants and any staff member with a mutual rapport/under-standing/likeability issue with any one student which is causing said student to be receiving a steady stream of detentions from said member of staff. Oh, and those tak-ing detention

Detention. What an evocative word. Who in the world, who has ever been to school, doesn't shy away from or bridle at that nine-letter word? 'For the act of [*insert example of childish misdemeanour*], we, Your School and Moral Guide, hereby detain, seize and hold you, stop you temporarily from proceeding with normal life, for the sum total of 30 minutes – an hour for serious stuff, two on Saturday for serial offenders.'

Detentions are set for all manner of reasons: for lateness and rudeness, laziness and forgetfulness; for swearing and bullying, defiance and dangerous behaviour. Sometimes they are issued as if out of a gun; at others, they come in slow-time, as if out of a pipette. Personally, I've preceded them with no warnings, one warning, two warnings and more; I've given informal and formal warnings; I've issued friendly ones and those more threatening; I've followed the school rules and I've completely failed to.

Rarely, however, whatever the occasion – apart from as some sort of misguided retribution – has it felt like the right thing to do. More an acceptance of defeat. A failure in me to bring about; through clever persuasion rather than stone-wall opposition, a better behaviour in someone else. Because as we know – not least because we know what it's like when the shoe is on the other foot – the humanely persuaded student, the one given help to retain control over their own self-destiny and free will, is generally far more positive and potent a force than the systematically, or arbitrarily, controlled one.

So, to my mind, the mere existence of detention is a failure of the system and all of us who are in it. We just don't have the time or the skills to deal with young people otherwise. But, even if heavily flawed, do detentions work?

A 2015 study by Dr Ruth Payne, a lecturer at Leeds University, who collated the findings of a detention questionnaire filled out by Year 7s and Year 11s in one UK secondary school, concluded, well, no. Although at pains to point out that there were 'a complex range of pupil responses to different behaviour management strategies', she was clear that 'sanctions such as asking pupils to miss break, or giving detentions, are seen to be counter-productive in encouraging pupils to work hard in class'.[1]

Indeed, as she told education journalist Nick Morrison, school discipline policies often rely on the popular think-ing that behaviour continues when it is reinforced and stops when it is not: 'That is great if you are training rats or pigeons but not when you are dealing with students,' she said. 'We don't take that approach in other areas of educa-tion so I don't know why we should have it in a behaviour policy.'[2]

---

1   R. Payne, Using rewards and sanctions in the classroom: pupils' perceptions of their own responses to current behaviour management strategies, *Educational Review*, 67(4) (2015): 483–504. See abstract at: https://www.tandfonline.com/doi/abs/10.1080/00131911.2015.1008407.

2   Quoted in N. Morrison, The surprising truth about discipline in schools, *Forbes* (31 August 2014). Available at: https://www.forbes.com/sites/nickmorrison/2014/08/31/the-surprising-truth-about-discipline-in-schools/#5fbc6e753f83.

That is not to say, I'm sure, that certain reinforcements, or dissuasions, don't work. But perhaps the nature of the reinforcement or dissuasion is what is key here – that taking away a child's freedom as a means of teaching them how to behave is at best simplistic. After all, there's no teaching involved other than the fact that 'If you do X, I'll do Y. And you won't like it. So don't.'

Which is all very well but, as you may now be screaming at the page, what else do students expect? And, in any case, how else are you meant to teach when 'Tiny' Matthews has tipped up his table for the fourth time this lesson and proceeded to shout 'Fuck the lot of you' at full volume from the vantage point of his chair? Tempt him down with marshmallows and a star of the week sticker?

'I don't even like fucking marshmallows!'

'Haribos do instead, Tiny?'

Less immediately satisfying but more subtle, surely – and, you would think, more effective long-term – are the schemes which still deny the child their freedom but, at the same time, enhance their behaviour by engaging with the reason behind their needing to be detained in the first place. I read of one example in which students were given a lunchtime detention with their teacher or head teacher, who used the opportunity not just to discuss the issue but also to get closer to the student, to understand them better. A social interaction with understanding at its heart but that still detains.[3]

---

3   E. Grazak, Lessons from lunch detention, *Education Week* (12 November 2013). Available at: https://www.edweek.org/ew/articles/2013/11/13/12grazek.h33.html, cited in S. McCann, Detention Is Not the Answer. Master's thesis, Northwestern College (2017). Available at: https://nwcommons.nwciowa.edu/cgi/viewcontent.cgi?article=1069&context=education_masters.

Name: .... Date: ....

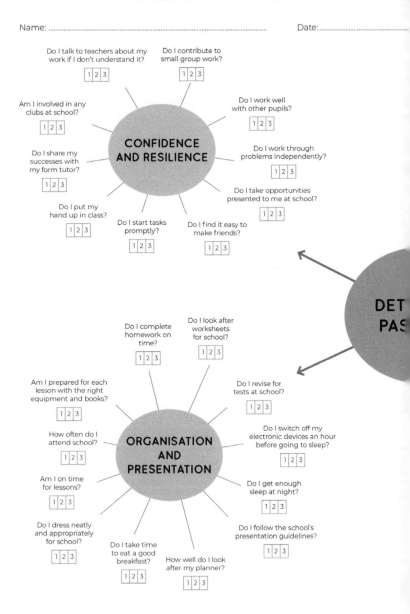

FIGURE 5. DETENTION PASSPORT

Note: Colour copies of the passport can be downloaded for free from:
https://www.crownhouse.co.uk/featured/emotional-literacy.

SETTING

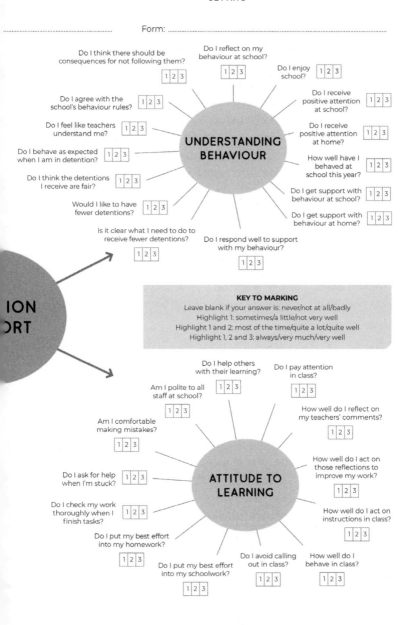

Do I think there should be consequences for not following them? `1` `2` `3`

Do I reflect on my behaviour at school? `1` `2` `3`

Do I enjoy school? `1` `2` `3`

Do I agree with the school's behaviour rules? `1` `2` `3`

Do I receive positive attention at school? `1` `2` `3`

Do I feel like teachers understand me? `1` `2` `3`

Do I receive positive attention at home? `1` `2` `3`

Do I behave as expected when I am in detention? `1` `2` `3`

UNDERSTANDING BEHAVIOUR

How well have I behaved at school this year? `1` `2` `3`

Do I think the detentions I receive are fair? `1` `2` `3`

Do I get support with behaviour at school? `1` `2` `3`

Would I like to have fewer detentions? `1` `2` `3`

Do I get support with behaviour at home? `1` `2` `3`

Is it clear what I need to do to receive fewer detentions? `1` `2` `3`

Do I respond well to support with my behaviour? `1` `2` `3`

KEY TO MARKING
Leave blank if your answer is: never/not at all/badly
Highlight 1: sometimes/a little/not very well
Highlight 1 and 2: most of the time/quite a lot/quite well
Highlight 1, 2 and 3: always/very much/very well

Do I help others with their learning? `1` `2` `3`

Do I pay attention in class? `1` `2` `3`

Am I polite to all staff at school? `1` `2` `3`

How well do I reflect on my teachers' comments? `1` `2` `3`

Am I comfortable making mistakes? `1` `2` `3`

ATTITUDE TO LEARNING

How well do I act on those reflections to improve my work? `1` `2` `3`

Do I ask for help when I'm stuck? `1` `2` `3`

Do I check my work thoroughly when I finish tasks? `1` `2` `3`

How well do I act on instructions in class? `1` `2` `3`

Do I put my best effort into my homework? `1` `2` `3`

Do I avoid calling out in class? `1` `2` `3`

How well do I behave in class? `1` `2` `3`

Do I put my best effort into my schoolwork? `1` `2` `3`

ION
ORT

Versions of this will already be happening in a good many schools up and down the country: the use of restorative measures to at least make best use of time spent in detention. If I were to guess, though, I'd suggest that even where such measures are in place, they will often lack the systemic and perhaps staff support to effect them well. That's my guess. We, the education system, believe that we have neither the capacity nor the intrinsic skills for restorative behavioural management – you know, helping kids to help themselves next time around, or even the time after that, or even the time 12 times after that. And even if we (the education system) did, we (a good many of us within it) are caught between believing in it and not really being sure – nor, of course, having enough time.

But the reality I've just guessed at will also be true for your use, should you choose to use it, of the detention passport (see Figure 5).

Nonetheless, you've got a captive audience (literally), and if it's true that the best change comes from the bottom up (in my head that's a proverb) then your work on it and, let's be positive, success with it, could just provoke a change in approach from which more students at your school could come to benefit.

I don't need to talk you through it. You know the drill. Choose your victim, rock up at detention, kindly request that you detain them at an alternative place of custody, whip out your passport, swallow any lingering pride or crumbs of vengeance, make and hold eye contact, and don't stop cajoling and co-working until you've both done your time. Just before discharge, arrange your next contact visit. Depending on the category of inmate, it could be back in detention in a week's time, which would be ideal, or in the case of the smaller-time offender, it might even have to be away from penitentiary. Regardless, use the visits or meetings to further your understanding of your student and, of course, theirs of themselves. Leave time in-between once you've established needs and how to meet needs. And use your new-found rapport to effect a change that sitting compulsorily, often angrily, in silence, for this particular child at least, has thus far failed to bring about.

OWEN

What is my need in understanding behaviour?

'I want support with behaviour at school.'

What I can do to meet this need:

'Ask to stand outside or calm down. Ask miss for a timeout card. Have a strategy for music lessons. Teach myself to get rid of the energy that makes me silly. Ask to have my counsellor back.'

My feelings about my efforts to meet my needs:

Week 1: 'I'm unhappy because I'm not allowed to have a timeout card. I feel like I don't want to get in trouble again like when I was messing around outside the art department and got an hour's detention.'

Week 2: 'Need to do less messing about and to ask to stand outside when I'm feeling silly.'

Week 3: 'Getting less negatives for shouting out. Doing better at that.'

Week 4: 'Happy with some improvements but not proud of my behaviour towards supply teachers and at lunch.'

Needs partly met ✓

Week 8 update: 'I'm so happy because I'm working with my counsellor again.'

CHAPTER 8
OUTCOMES

The passport has had many different guises over the years, such was the need to keep evolving it into something more useful for students than it was previously. It has been high-lighted in a rainbow of different colours, it has been filled in with good faith and with flippancy, and it has been used to express pride and show disgust. But the one constant that has remained are the students who have brought it to life. Here, then, is a brief look at how some of those we've met fared with its use.

MILENA

Who needed *to talk to her teachers more* and also *to get enough sleep at night*:

- Was surprised at how useful it was talking to her English teacher about her work.

- Was then moved to a new seat, following further useful conversations, which she said 'helped with my concentration'.

- Began enjoying lessons more and making good progress.

- While also starting to sleep better with her new penchant for audiobooks.

- And observing that 'not all books are bad' and 'you can find anything interesting if you try hard'.

- And, just for the record, while trying to *help others with their learning*, 'helped my partner on a project and brought it home to finish' and felt 'really happy for doing that'.

JORDAN

Who having succeeded in *contributing to small group work*, needed to then *complete homework on time*:

- Spent four weeks trying to get to morning homework club.

- With a variety of inventive reasons for not making it.

- And tried in-between but conceded on week 4, 'I'm not completing all of my homework', concluding he would need to 'try harder next time'.

- He finally managed to get to homework club somewhere during week 8.

- And was delighted to finish one piece of homework.

- He came again the next day and, with the help of those there, finished another.

- And then couldn't stop attending.

- Which was all the more impressive because he wasn't even interested in the breakfast provided.

- He started gaining more commendations than he did detentions.

- And was last seen running off to the science department to hand in yet another piece of completed homework (on time).

BRANDON

Who, over the space of several years, needed *to share his successes with his form tutor:*

- Started school unable to read a basic text or to write legibly.

- Struggled with friendship groups and with teachers.

- And in no way did he want to share his successes because he felt like 'a failure at everything'.

- However, he did once let on that he'd 'shot four nets in netball'.

- And 'picked up badges' at Scouts.

- He also practised reading, over and over, a series of books he could barely read, but did so because he so 'loved the characters'.

- An ongoing success which he shared and shared again.

- He also had the courage one day to read out loud in English and 'loved it'.

- A success which he also shared with his tutor.

- And was last seen with a big smile on his face having just passed his English exams.

And finally, a look at some we've not yet met.

BARTEK

Who, over the course of several passports, needed to *check work thoroughly* and *talk to teachers about his work:*

● Started by reading over a paragraph of writing in literacy intervention.

● Moved on to checking over literacy work each week.

● And then to checking back over English assessments and discussing them with his teacher.

● One day he really enjoyed reading out loud a play by a well-known playwright.

● So continued to read the whole play, together with his friend.

● Next he thoroughly checked over the letter he co-wrote to the author to share his comments and thoughts.

● And was shocked when the playwright replied. Kindly. And in detail.

● He told his English teacher about receiving a letter from a playwright.

● Who shared it with his head of year, who shared it with the head.

● Who congratulated him in person and gave him an award.

● An outcome which he shared with his new playwright friend, to say thank you – while again checking the letter thoroughly.

- He told him he 'felt great' because his letter had given him 'more confidce in English litrecher' and wished him well for his future work.

- He was a boy with dyslexia.

DRAKE

Who also, over the course of several passports, needed to *put his hand up more in class* and *check his work thoroughly:*

- So he tried 'not to worry about being wrong from time to time'.

- And started by putting his hand up in French

- He gradually moved on to also doing so in RE, DT, geography, history and maths.

- And won an award for the most improved student in geography.

- During literacy intervention classes, he (also) really enjoyed reading out loud a play by a famous playwright.

- And also thoroughly checked the letter he co-wrote to him to share his comments and thoughts.

- He was even more shocked when the playwright replied. Kindly. And in detail.

- And also shared with his English teacher his success of receiving a letter from a playwright.

- Who shared it with his head of year, who shared it with the head.

- Who congratulated him in person and gave him an award.

- An event which he also shared with his new playwright friend, to say thank you – while again checking his letter carefully.

- He told him he 'wasn't expecting [him] to write back' but that it made him 'feel more confident in English tuition'. And that he 'got to see the head teacher all because of you'.

- He worked his socks off at school, despite some key learning barriers, and was rewarded with the results that enabled him to go on to do what he wanted to do next.

YUSRA

Who needed *to complete her homework on time* while also *avoiding calling out in class*:

- She set her alarm for 7am every morning to check her homework was packed in her bag.

- And also determined to explain to sir why she was calling out in geography.

- She found that the alarm (system) started working as early as week 1.

- And found the same for her new system in geography – putting her hand up more.

- She found she was getting fewer detentions for missing homework by week 2.

- And was also getting fewer detentions – but more positives – in geography.

- She got herself a new folder in week 3 which helped her to be even more organised.

- And was also continuing to call out less in geography.

- She'd had no homework detentions for a month by week 4, even though her phone had 'lost battery' and the 'alarm broke' but thankfully is 'fixed now'.

- She decided she had 'changed behaviour from calling out to putting my hand up' with 'no negatives for calling out'.

- She concluded her needs were partly met for bringing her homework in on time and met for not calling out.

- She told her teacher, who told her parents, who were delighted – which encouraged her even more at school.

BROOKE

Who, on and off over the course of her secondary education, needed to *share her successes with her form tutor* and many other passport issues besides:

- She began and finished school with few friends, but she was inseparable from the ones she made.

- She taught herself how best to cope with bullies, who knew she was different.

- She didn't care much for homework.

- She didn't care much for school rules.

- She knew certain swear words and wasn't afraid to use them.

- She struggled to stay in most of her classes, for most of her schooling, because of issues of non-compliance.

- But she attended every single parents' evening with her mum.

- She dressed neatly for school – for the start of it, anyway.

- She didn't need to be taught Shakespeare – she innately got it (they would have been mates, in fact).

- Ultimately, she achieved some very good grades, including English.

- And shared some of these successes with her tutor.

- She was humorous, a gifted thinker and also empathic.

- When she was older, she wanted to be a counsellor for autistic children.

- She was a girl with autism attending a state secondary school.

FINAL THOUGHTS

The passport may have started life as a conversation between two teachers, but its early years have clearly been lived as a dialogue between teacher and pupil. One that hopefully does what all good dialogue should – share information, offer perspective, afford subtlety, imbue honesty. And, where needed, inspire action and, in turn, change.

It may not be for you. It may not be for your pupils. If all roads do indeed lead to Rome, there will be many different ways of tackling the issues the passport raises and you may already be very much on top of them – in a way that suits your schedule, your working style, your pupils.

Or it may be that by discussing it, and the issues it throws up, you find different solutions or systems that are much more snug a fit with your school.

But if none of those are you and if – without even asking a responsible adult – you've thrown on your cozzie, strapped your goggles on your head and are shivering with anticipation at poolside, then you appear to be ready to dive straight in. In which case, my final thoughts are as follows:

● This is now your passport – not mine. Print it, change it, keep it, share it.[1] Do whatever you like with it, but make it yours. To suit you. Your school. Your pupils.

● Stick it in front of someone's nose to approve and give them your reasons. They will; you've got your cozzie on. What are they going to do – tell you to change?

---

1   Colour copies of the passport can be downloaded for free from: https://www.crownhouse.co.uk/featured/emotional-literacy.

- Get the time – proper time, not tea-break time – alongside the approval. This isn't a quick splash-around.

- Choose your setting (Chapter 7), choose your pupil (Chapter 3), check the system (Chapter 3), choose your start time.

- Listen, talk, listen and be merry. And be sad. And all things in-between.

- And when things don't go how you wanted, that's par for the course. At first, and maybe second. Stick with it. It will deliver. No slinking off to the changing rooms.

The idea of this book was to share an idea; thank you for being shared with. It was also to raise the notion that school – for all its brilliance in the year 2020, for all the noble and genuinely inspiring things that happen in its midst and in its cause – is still missing a vital foundation: the one that educates pupils in how to manage themselves and their emotions, in order to manage school itself. In short, to know that their first school essential isn't bought from a shop or online; it isn't too short, too long or too baggy; it is something acquired at school itself: it is their emotional literacy, to be tapped into and excited. And it starts on day one.

REFERENCES AND FURTHER READING

Ackerman, C. E. (2020) What is self-esteem? A psychologist explains, *Positive Psychology* (16 April). Available at: https://positivepsychology.com/self-esteem.

Adams, R. (2017) Exeter school's uniform resolve melts after boys' skirt protest, *The Guardian* (23 June). Available at: https://www.theguardian.com/education/2017/jun/23/exeter-schools-uniform-resolve-melts-after-boys-skirt-protest.

Adolphus, K., Lawton, C. L. and Dye, L. (2019) Associations between habitual school-day breakfast consumption frequency and academic performance in British adolescents, *Frontiers in Public Health*, 7: 283. Available at: https://www.frontiersin.org/articles/10.3389/fpubh.2019.00283/full.

American Academy of Sleep Medicine (2008) Poor sleep can negatively affect a student's grades, increase the odds of emotional and behavioral disturbance [press release] (9 June). Available at: https://aasm.org/poor-sleep-can-negatively-affect-a-students-grades-increase-the-odds-of-emotional-and-behavioral-disturbance.

Bradford, E. (2013) Half of teenagers sleep deprived, say experts, *BBC News* (26 August). Available at: https://www.bbc.co.uk/news/uk-scotland-23811690.

Britton, J., Farquharson, C. and Sibieta, L. (2019) *2019 Annual Report on Education Spending in England* (London: Institute for Fiscal Studies). Available at: https://www.ifs.org.uk/uploads/R162-Education-spending-in-England-2019.pdf.

Brown, T. E. (2016) ADHD Explained: A 28-Minute Primer [video], *Understood.com*. Available at: https://www.understood.org/en/learning-thinking-differences/child-learning-disabilities/add-adhd/adhd-explained-a-28-minute-primer?_ul=1*6w1pkr*domain_userid*YW1wLVNsdERGczl6SGluZlFJS0tVU2VZX0E.

Busch, B. (2016) The science of revision: nine ways pupils can revise for exams more effectively, *The Guardian* (19 April). Available at: https://www.theguardian.com/teacher-network/2016/apr/19/students-revise-exams-revision-science.

Chief Secretary to the Treasury (2003) *Every Child Matters*, Cm. 5860 (London: TSO). Available at: https://www.gov.uk/government/publications/every-child-matters.

Children's Society (2019) *The Good Childhood Report 2019*. Available at: https://www.childrenssociety.org.uk/sites/default/files/the_good_childhood_report_2019.pdf.

Coe, R., Aloisi, C., Higgins, S. and Elliot Major, L. (2014) *What Makes Great Teaching? Review of the Underpinning Research* (London: Sutton Trust). Available at: https://www.suttontrust.com/wp-content/uploads/2019/12/What-makes-great-teaching-FINAL-4.11.14-1.pdf.

Cohen, D. (2013) Revision techniques – the good, the OK and the useless, *BBC News* (18 May). Available at: https://www.bbc.co.uk/news/health-22565912.

Cowburn, A. and Blow, M. (2017) *Wise Up: Prioritising Wellbeing in Schools* (London: Young Minds). Available at: https://youngminds.org.uk/media/1428/wise-up-prioritising-wellbeing-in-schools.pdf.

Department for Education (2014) *Influences on Students' GCSE Attainment and Progress at Age 16: Effective Pre-school, Primary & Secondary Education Project (EPPSE)*. Research Report (September). Available at: https://assets.publishing.service.gov.uk/government/uploads/system/uploads/attachment_data/file/373286/RR352_-_Influences_on_Students_GCSE_Attainment_and_Progress_at_Age_16.pdf.

Department for Education (2019a) Permanent and fixed period exclusions in England: 2017 to 2018 (25 July). Available at: https://assets.publishing.service.gov.uk/government/uploads/system/uploads/attachment_data/file/820773/Permanent_and_fixed_period_exclusions_2017_to_2018_-_main_text.pdf.

Department for Education (2019b) Pupil absence in schools in England: 2017 to 2018 (21 March). Available at: https://assets.publishing.service.gov.uk/government/uploads/system/uploads/attachment_data/file/787463/Absence_3term_201718_Text.pdf.

Durlak, J. A., Weissberg, R. P., Dymnicki, A. B., Taylor, R. B. and Schellinger, K. B. (2011) The impact of enhancing students' social and emotional learning: a meta-analysis of school-based universal interventions, *Child Development*, 82(1): 405–432. Available at: http://www.casel.org/wp-content/uploads/2016/01/meta-analysis-child-development-1.pdf.

Dweck, C. S. (2012) *Mindset: How You Can Fulfil Your Potential* (London: Constable & Robinson).

French, H. (2017) What are we doing to our children?, *The Telegraph* (10 October). Available at: https://www.telegraph.co.uk/education/2017/10/10/children1.

Gilbert, I. (2007) *The Little Book of Thunks: 260 Questions to Make Your Brain Go Ouch!* (Carmarthen: Crown House Publishing).

Goleman, D. (1996) *Emotional Intelligence: Why It Can Matter More Than IQ* (London: Bloomsbury).

Grazak, E. (2013) Lessons from lunch detention, *Education Week* (12 November). Available at: https://www.edweek.org/ew/articles/2013/11/13/12grazek.h33.html.

Gunnars, K. (2019) Blue light and sleep: what's the connection?, *Healthline* (28 January). Available at: https://www.healthline.com/nutrition/block-blue-light-to-sleep-better.

Hutchinson, J. and Crenna-Jennings, W. (2019) *Unexplained Pupil Exits from Schools: A Growing Problem?* Working paper (April) (London: Education Policy Institute). Available at: https://epi.org.uk/wp-content/uploads/2019/04/EPI_Unexplained-pupil-exits_2019.pdf.

Hurley, C. (ed) (1997) *Could Do Better: School Reports of the Great and the Good* (London: Simon and Schuster).

Institute of Student Employers (ISE) (2020) Graduate Jobs Decline in 21 Countries Due to Covid-19, *FE News* (15 July). Available at: https://www.fenews.co.uk/press-releases/51463-graduate-jobs-decline-in-21-countries-due-to-covid-19.

Issimdar, M. (2018) Homeschooling in the UK increases 40% over three years, *BBC News* (26 April). Available at: https://www.bbc.co.uk/news/uk-england-42624220.

Kelly, J. (2012) The learning pyramid, *Peak Performance Center* (September). Available at: https://thepeakperformancecenter. com/educational-learning/learning/principles-of-learning/ learning-pyramid.

Kumar, P. P. (2009) *My Time, My World* (Kindle Edition).

Littlecott, H. J., Moore, G. F., Moore, L. and Lyons, R. A. (2016) Association between breakfast consumption and educational outcomes in 9–11-year-old children, *Public Health Nutrition*, 19(9): 1575–1582.

McCann, S. (2017) Detention Is Not the Answer. Master's thesis, Northwestern College. Available at: https://nwcommons.nwciowa. edu/cgi/viewcontent.cgi?article=1069&context=education_ masters.

Makortoff, K. (2020) UK Employers Will Offer Fewer Entry-Level Jobs in 2020, Figures Suggest, *The Guardian* (6 January). Available at: https://www.theguardian.com/money/2020/jan/06/ uk-employers-fewer-entry-level-jobs-2020-survey.

Morrison, N. (2014) The surprising truth about discipline in schools, *Forbes* (31 August). Available at: https://www.forbes.com/ sites/nickmorrison/2014/08/31/the-surprising-truth-about-discipline-in-schools/#5fbc6e753f83.

OECD (2017) *PISA 2015 Results (Volume III): Students' Well-being* (Paris: OECD Publishing). Available at: https://www.oecd.org/pisa/ PISA-2015-Results-Students-Well-being-Volume-III-Overview.pdf.

Ofqual (2019) Guide to GCSE results for England, 2019 [press release] (22 August). Available at: https://www.gov.uk/ government/news/guide-to-gcse-results-for-england-2019.

Payne, R. (2015) Using rewards and sanctions in the classroom: pupils' perceptions of their own responses to current behaviour management strategies, *Educational Review*, 67(4): 483–504.

Perham N. and Currie, H. (2014) Does listening to preferred music improve reading comprehension performance?, *Applied Cognitive Psychology*, 28(2): 279–284. Available at: https:// onlinelibrary.wiley.com/doi/abs/10.1002/acp.2994.

Prooday, V. (2017) When children are disorganized: reasons & solutions (2 November). Available at: https://yourot.com/parenting-club/2017/11/22/when-children-are-disorganized-reasons-solutions.

Ro, C. (2018) Why sleep should be every student's priority, *BBC Future* (20 August). Available at: https://www.bbc.com/future/article/20180815-why-sleep-should-be-every-students-priority.

Rosenshine, B. (2012) Principles of instruction: research-based strategies that all teachers should know, *American Educator*, 36(1): 12–19, 39.

Ryback, R. (2016) The powerful psychology behind cleanliness: how to stay organized, and reap the health benefits, *Psychology Today* (11 July). Available at: https://www.psychologytoday.com/us/blog/the-truisms-wellness/201607/the-powerful-psychology-behind-cleanliness.

TUC (2019) Workers in the UK put in more than £32 billion worth of unpaid overtime last year [press release] (1 March). Available at: https://www.tuc.org.uk/news/workers-uk-put-more-£32-billion-worth-unpaid-overtime-last-year-tuc-analysis.

Ward, H. (2017) New Pisa happiness table: see where UK pupils rank, *TES* (19 April). Available at: https://www.tes.com/news/new-pisa-happiness-table-see-where-uk-pupils-rank.

Weale, S. (2015) Missing lessons harms children's education, says UK government, *The Guardian* (22 February). Available at: https://www.theguardian.com/education/2015/feb/22/missing-lessons-harms-childrens-education-uk-government.

World Economic Forum (2018) *The Future of Jobs Report 2018* (Insight Report) (Geneva: World Economic Forum). Available at: http://www3.weforum.org/docs/WEF_Future_of_Jobs_2018.pdf.

978-178135337-0

978-178135338-7

978-178135339-4

978-178135340-0

978-178135341-7

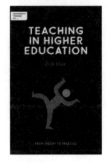

978-178135369-1

978-178135373-8

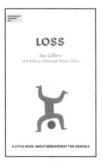

978-178135353-0

independent thinking press

www.independentthinkingpress.com

ındependent thinking

Independent Thinking. An education company.

Taking people's brains for a walk since 1994.

We use our words.

www.independentthinking.com